a **better** financial plan

SIGNIFICANTLY IMPROVE YOUR FINANCES
WITHOUT THE HELP OF WALL STREET

SECOND EDITION

DEAN J. VAGNOZZI

1346
PUBLISHING
COLLEGEVILLE, PA

Published by
1346 Publishing
Collegeville, PA

Publisher's Cataloging-in-Publication Data
Vagnozzi, Dean J.

A better financial plan : significantly improve your finances without the help of Wall Street / Dean J. Vagnozzi. - 2nd. ed. - Collegeville, PA : 1346 Pub., 2018.

p. ; cm.

ISBN13: 978-0-9973786-2-7

1. Finance, Personal--United States. 2. Retirement--United States--Planning. 3. 401(k) plans. 5. Investments. I. Title.

HG179.V35 2018
332.02401—dc23   2018908777

SECOND EDITION

Interior design by Brooke Camfield

Printed in the United States of America

22   21   20   19   18   •   5   4   3   2   1

Dedication

To my family, starting with my parents, Fiore and Anita Vagnozzi. You both worked multiple jobs while I was growing up to provide for your family. From you both, I learned something that cannot be taught in any school: work ethic! I hope to pass this characteristic on to my four children. Thank you. To my kids, Alec, Gabrielle, Mitchell, and Felicia, you mean the world to me. You will always be my greatest accomplishment. Most of all, I dedicate this book to my beautiful wife of 25 years, Christa. You are without question the best listener, friend, mother, and wife a guy could ever ask for. I wouldn't be able to achieve a thing professionally if it weren't for your emotional support and encouragement and the fact that I knew all was well at home because of you. Thank you for all that you do taking care of our family. I love you.

Contents

Acknowledgments

This book was written due to the overwhelmingly positive response and encouragement that I've received from my financial education seminar attendees since 2004, as well as hundreds of advisors who have heard my message since then. Oh, and my sister, Dana, strongly encouraged me, too.

As you will learn more about in the following chapters, I made a 180-degree career change in 2004. My wife, Christa, and I had just moved into a new home and had our fourth child. One day I came home and said I wanted to become a financial advisor. OK, a few things happened that led me to come to that conclusion, as you will learn soon enough, but that is kind of what happened. I could not have picked a riskier time in my life to leave my steady income to get into a career in which I had no experience, no clients, no health benefits, and no income. What I did have was passion, confidence, and my amazing wife, Christa, who believed in me. Yes, she was nervous. Yes, she was scared. But she believed in me, and she was extremely supportive. Looking back, I see it was the craziest thing I ever did—or ever will do—in my lifetime. Ninety-nine percent of spouses would have said no way! But not Christa. That career change has allowed me to find my passion and along the way help so many people secure their finances. None of that would have happened if it weren't for Christa's encouragement and support.

Robert Castiglione and his company Leap Systems need recognition too. Bob, is the Babe Ruth of the financial services industry. He retired a few years ago. As I transitioned to my new career, I attended many training classes, seminars and conferences conducted by Bob and his staff at Leap. These sessions helped me look at financial planning in a whole new light. I left their events invigorated, inspired and enthusiastic about helping as many people as I could improve their finances. I've without question put my own spin on the things I learned from Bob and Leap . . . a few significant spins I should stress…but the foundation to much of what you read in this book I learned from Bob and his company. Bob and I have become good friends over the years and at the time of this writing I have NEVER beaten him at golf.

Mary Ann Lacey-Gray is another person I owe a lot of thanks too. If Bob Castiglione is the Babe Ruth of the financial services business, then Mary Ann Lacey-Gray is the Amelia Earhart. When I first jumped into the financial services business, I was on my own, literally! I needed help. Mary Ann and her company Underwriters Marketing Service act as the back office for advisors around the country, which is exactly what she did for me. This allowed me to focus on my customers. In an industry that is dominated by men, Mary Ann Lacey-Gray provides her clients the personal touch that only a woman knows how to do. She's become a trusted mentor over the years and a close friend. Mary Ann is as excited about my success as any non-family member can be. Thank you Mary Ann for all you have done for me.

I'd also like to give a big thank you to my good friend Joel Capperella. Not only is Joel someone I've known since high school but he is also a client. Over the years Joel has taken a strong interest in my business and has helped me get my word out utilizing social media and other marketing efforts. It took a long time to write—and rewrite—this book. About eight months to be exact. During that time, I occasionally struggled to find the words to help deliver my message. That's when I would bounce things off of Joel and he would help me articulate my thoughts into words. Had it not been for Joel, this book would have taken months longer to complete. Again, thank you, Joel.

chapter 1

A Financial Life Preserver

If you want A Better Financial Plan, then you've come to the right place. This book is going to show you how to significantly improve your retirement planning. Not slightly improve it—*significantly* improve it! This book will help you regardless of whether you are 20, 35, 50, or 70 years of age. Consider this book a life preserver for your financial plan. The dilemma for you is whether you want to grab it or push it away. The first thing I'm going to do is rip to shreds the logic of traditional financial planning, so brace yourself. When I mention traditional financial planning, I am primarily talking about the 401(k) and IRA. In order to improve your financial plan, you have to first realize the shortcomings of what you are likely doing with your money. Only then can I help improve your finances. If my logic doesn't make sense after you read the first three chapters, then put the book down, because I doubt that you will be open to the suggestions I make in the remaining chapters.

Do you realize that just 3% of the US population is financially independent? Just 3%. Do you think this 3% of people are doing the same thing with their money as the other 97%? Of course not. You know they are not. I need you to think and invest like the 3%, not the 97%. Keep that in mind as we proceed.

Let me tell you now that I'm not a fan of the 401(k) or traditional IRA. Each is an investment vehicle for the 97%, not the 3%. Roth IRAs are a step in the right direction, but they too are severely flawed. If you have children and you are saving for their college education, then you've likely been told to put money into a college 529 plan. Another move for the 97%. Do you have a 15-year mortgage or shorter? Are you sending extra money each month on your 30-year mortgage? How about a biweekly mortgage? Do you have any of the above? These are all strategies implemented by the 97%. I'll tell you why they are flawed soon enough.

I hope you are the type of person who is open to new ideas and is willing to zig (3%) when everyone else zags (97%), so long as the logic makes sense. When you implement what you learn in this book, your rewards will be A Better Financial Plan that does the following for you:

- Provides increased liquidity.

- As a result of your increased liquidity, better protects you from any unexpected financial hardships that may arise.

- Will deliver a good rate of return on your long-term savings.

- Results in your paying less in taxes during retirement—a lot less in taxes!

- Allows you to pay less in fees to traditional advisors.

- Dramatically reduces the amount of time you spend managing your retirement plan.

- As a result of all of the above, positions you to spend and enjoy 30%–50% more money during retirement than if you stay on the path taught by most traditional advisors.

The best part is this: you will learn how to accomplish all of the above while *reducing* your overall investment risk and without changing your cash flow one bit. Oh, and the solution isn't complicated. It's easy. After all, the best things in life usually are. Sound too good to be true? Perhaps it does, but if you do your research, you'll find that hundreds of thousands of people around the country have been implementing the strategies that you will learn throughout this book for years, and the numbers are growing by the tens of thousands each year. So although what you are about to learn may be new to you, I assure you that you are not the guinea pig.

Let me also point out what this book won't do for you. It won't help you formulate a comprehensive financial plan or help you properly allocate and diversify all of your assets. That would be impossible for me or anyone else to do without thoroughly understanding your personal situation. I laugh when I stumble upon Dave Ramsey or Suze Orman on the radio or a local cable channel, or any other advisor for that matter, dishing out all of this "one-size-fits-all" financial advice to people without knowing all of the facts about each listener's financial situation. That is impossible to do for any advisor. I'm not attempting to do that in this book.

So, wait a minute: I just got done telling you this book will show you how to significantly improve your finances, and now I'm telling you I can't help you with a comprehensive financial plan. Which is it? It's both! As I said, the first thing you are going to learn is what is wrong with traditional financial planning. When you understand all of its shortcomings, you will likely want to redirect or reallocate some if not all of your long-term savings. I will then spend the rest of the book covering one specific financial strategy *that if implemented* will make more of a positive impact on your long-term retirement savings than anything else you can do. Anything! That being said, are there other things you can do with your savings that will complement the strategy that you learn here even more? Absolutely, but none will have a greater, more positive impact on your finances than what you learn in the following chapters, and I intend to prove it.

What I cover in this book is completely based on and illustrated with facts. There are plenty of "opinion" books out there. I assure you this won't be another one of them. After all, you know what they say about opinions. I'm going to back up every statement I make in this book with proof to support my claims. This way, the next time someone gives you some financial advice that contradicts what you learn in the pages that follow, you'll be able to confidently ignore his or her flawed wisdom. Better yet, give that person a copy of this book to read so that he or she can see the light as well. Then *you'll* be the one throwing the financial life preserver.

So who am I, and what qualifies me as someone from whom you should be taking advice? I'll give you some basic information now, but I admit it may seem vague. My qualifications will be told throughout the following chapters, because my financial success is a direct result of implementing what you are about to learn. This book, in essence, is my résumé. You'll see what I mean as we go.

In 2003 I started my financial planning practice in a town called King of Prussia, Pennsylvania, about 15 miles west of Philadelphia. I have an accounting degree from Albright College, a small liberal arts college in Reading, Pennsylvania. I am 50 years old and have been happily married to the same woman since 1993. We have four beautiful children between the ages of 15 and 22.

I became a financial professional because I experienced firsthand the pitfalls of traditional planning. I have also greatly benefited from the strategy that you will learn about in this book. I was a student before I became a teacher. To date I have thousands of clients who have successfully implemented everything you will learn in the chapters ahead. I deliver weekly financial seminars all over the country to audiences ranging from 25 to 200. Every seminar is the same, and so are the reactions of my attendees. I start by pointing out the flaws of traditional planning. The facial expressions of my attendees are priceless. "I've never heard it explained that way before" is something I've heard 10 times a week since 2003. I've also been told to write a book a thousand times as well. I'm finally doing it.

I'm a "street-smart" financial professional with real-life game experience. I know what it is like to do a fantastic job of saving my money during the '90s only to feel the pain of watching my wealth get decimated by a stock market correction, as was the case from 2000 to 2002. I've lent money to friends and family only to never see it come back. I've purchased cash-value life insurance from my friends just to get them to leave me alone. I own a bunch of gold. I've watched its value soar, only to see it drop dramatically the past couple of years. Do you notice you don't see the gold commercials on television much anymore? I've done the real estate thing too. I've easily made over a million dollars investing in real estate from 2000 to 2008. I also know what it's like to have a third of my rental units sit vacant for months at a time or to get the phone call from my property manager telling me there has been a fire in one of my units. Talk about stress. Today, I have other investments worth several million dollars that were derived from the liquidity of my long-term savings and my ability to seize the moment when business opportunities arose. More on that later. Most people you see or hear giving financial advice on radio or television *don't have financial game experience*. In fact, very few financial advisors with Merrill Lynch, Edward Jones, Morgan Stanley, Ameriprise, or ANY other brokerage firm, for that matter, have financial game experience. Neither do most accountants, attorneys, or bankers. Most advisors of any type haven't taken a financial risk in their life. Most are in no better shape financially than their clients; many, in fact, are in worse financial shape. I am not exaggerating one bit on that statement. Whatever money they have made is a result of their job and not the result of investment successes that they have had.

From whom do you want to take financial advice? The financial professional who has made his or her money solely from the fees and commissions collected from clients? Or the professional who has made a lot of money with investments and business opportunities that he or she has participated in, as well as the income derived from running a successful financial planning firm? I sure hope you'd prefer to take advice from someone who has made significant money from his or her investments and not just the fees or commissions he or she charges clients.

Again, it is my experience that very few advisors have made true wealth in anything outside of their practice. Don't believe me? Put your advisor on the spot and ask him or her. It's a fair question. After all, your advisor asks you about your finances, right? It's OK for you to ask, but very few clients do, so you will probably catch him or her off guard. Watch your advisor become speechless when you ask him or her to provide a list of financial successes he or she has had outside of his or her practice.

OK, enough already. Like I said, you'll find out more about me as we go. Now it's time to learn a better financial plan. I'm about to throw you a life preserver. Get ready to grab it.

chapter 2

The 401(k) and IRA, the Other Side of the Story

I'm about to trash traditional planning, in particular the 401(k) and IRA. There is no other way to put it. I'm going to do so over the next two chapters, taking a different angle in each. In this chapter I'm going to point out the flaws pertaining to how these plans are relied on for retirement planning. The next chapter will look at the characteristics of the 401(k) and IRA as pure investment vehicle chassis. The merits of each view stand on their own. When you combine them, "Forget about it," as many of us Italians say when something is a no-brainer.

I don't think I've ever been so excited about putting something in writing as I was when working on the next two chapters. You won't implement any of my suggestions on how to improve your finances unless I can help you understand what is wrong with traditional planning, which is what I've set out to do in the following sections.

If you are still working and saving money for retirement, then reading the next two chapters is a must. Imagine that there is a 10-mile traffic jam on the highway. This book is going to show you the detour to avoid the financial logjam up ahead. If you are retired and not contributing to a 401(k) or IRA anymore, I still want you to read the next two chapters, because you will likely say to yourself, "Yeah, he is spot-on. Why couldn't I have learned this 30 years ago?" You, too, Mr. or Mrs. Retired Person, will majorly benefit from the following chapters, but you will take my suggestions more seriously if I can impress you with my views on traditional planning. Here we go.

The Perfect Retirement

I want you to take a moment to think about what your perfect retirement looks like. Think for a minute or two of what you'd like your financial status to be in that period of your life. If you are like most, the vision of your retirement, financially speaking, has you living in a home that you have paid off years before, a home that holds plenty of memories of raising your now grown children. You are drawing on your 401(k), getting a little bit of Social Security, and living the lifestyle that you'd hoped for—traveling when you want, visiting the grandchildren often, and exploring things that you'd hoped you'd explore once you got here.

But what if I told you that the road you are currently on, the road that you decided to take to your financial future, was backed up for miles and miles because of some unforeseen problem ahead? If that were true, would you want to know immediately—I mean, would you want to know that this was the case right now, today, without delay?

Of course you would. It is sort of like when you hit the road on vacation and you have a pretty solid four- or five-hour drive ahead of you. If the main route you are going to take is stopped dead because of a jackknifed tractor-trailer, you want to know about it far before you hit the traffic, don't you? Again, of course you do. You'd want to know so that you can take an alternative route. In fact, you'd be happy to add more miles onto your trip if it meant that you could keep moving forward rather than just stop dead with no progress.

Well, I do have bad news for you, I'm afraid. The single most popular retirement plan in the United States is sort of like that backed-up route to your vacation destination. There's a problem ahead, and you need to adjust course now in order to account for the problem. You need to examine an alternative route and take it so that the flaws of the status quo retirement savings plan don't keep you from reaching that perfect retirement we mentioned just a couple of paragraphs ago.

A Brief History of the 401(k)

Why is it even called a 401(k)? Seriously, do we even know what those numbers and one letter represent? If you don't know where the name comes from, you are not alone. The term 401(k) represents section 401(k) of the Internal Revenue Code written in 1978. So let's take a look at why the 401(k) was created, the environment in which it was created, and why the fact that it was never designed to be the sole source of retirement planning in the United States is problematic for those of us living in the twenty-first century.

Before we dive in here, I want to properly set your expectations. I'm going to give you just some cursory history here. There are obviously nuances to the evolution of the 401(k), and there are some benefits. But the reality is that the dependency that the US population has today on the 401(k) as a main savings vehicle was never intended to be. And that is the point. Since the early '80s an entire industry has evolved to exploit a section of IRS code that was originally intended for something completely different.

Section 401(k) of the Internal Revenue Code was added primarily as a compromise between the federal government's desire to tax high-income earners and high-income earners' desire to decrease their income tax rate as much as possible. The original language of the code allowed employers to decrease profits in a manner that would decrease, or, rather, defer, their tax burden. In 1980, an employee benefits consultant by the name of Ted Benna noticed that the code could potentially allow employees to take a similar advantage. This would incent employers to provide a mechanism for employees to elect to defer some of their income into these newly created plans. On behalf of his employer, Mr. Benna petitioned the IRS to modify 401, section k, to allow such funds to be created. In 1981 the code was amended, and as early as 1983, there were seven million 401(k) participants; as of 2014 (according to the Investment Company Institute, Federal Reserve Board, and Department of Labor), there is over $4.4 trillion (yes, with a *t*) tied up in 401(k) plans. This represents almost a quarter of all retirement assets in the entire United States.

So here we are 40 years after the dawn of the 401(k), and the landscape has been radically changed for the average American. In the late '70s and early '80s, nearly 80% of all laborers in the United States had a pension plan as part of their entire compensation package. In addition, there was almost no talk about the solvency of the Social Security program. So, in effect, the 401(k) was ADDING on to what had been the established long-term financial plan for nearly everyone across the entire country since World War II. Read that sentence again because it is important. The 401(k) was an addition to the prevailing wisdom of long-term savings at the time.

Fast-forward now to the second decade of the new millennium and it is a different environment. Many of our political leaders believe that Social Security will be insolvent in the 2030s if nothing is done to address the strains on the system's current infrastructure. Today, fewer than 10% of employees have any sort of pension plan on which to depend. The 401(k) was the third leg to a retirement savings strategy stool; now, for most people, it is the only leg.

The Stock Market Is Risky

One of the major problems with the ever-increasing dependency on the 401(k) is that at its heart, it is a stock-market-driven approach. Of course, 401(k) investors have options to move their money into safe vehicles, but by doing so, they forfeit any hope of growth. To ensure growth, the average investor believes he or she has no choice but to endure market risk. Accepting this risk is sold by the financial planning industry by telling them, "Don't worry; over time you'll perform just fine at about 8%–10%. After all, that is the historical return of the market."

Sounds fair, right? Stick it out, hold on for the ride, don't worry about losses, and by the end you're gonna get yourself 8%–10% on your investment. Seriously, this is how the market is sold to us today: just buy and hold, buy and hold. That is the "strategy" that is going to net you very comfortable growth.

What is true about this? Well, it depends on the time we are examining. It is true that, historically, the market does 8%–10%, BUT that is typically over an 80–90-year window. **Eighty years!** Who has 80 years to invest? Most people reading this book have a 10-, 20-, 30-, or 40-year investment horizon. And there are plenty of 10-, 20-, 30-, or 40-year time frames that the market hasn't moved. I will prove that a few times in the upcoming chapters. So let's consider a more realistic example.

If we look at market performance since it hit its bottom on March 9, 2009, we happily realize that the S&P 500 has returned about 16% through December 31, 2015. In fact, the market is on the best bull run in its history at the time of this writing. But that 16% growth looks great only if we erase our memory of the 20%, 30%, or even 40% decline we experienced in 2008.

Let's put this in perspective. Suppose a 45-year-old woman on the first business day of January 2000 finally reaches the point in her earning life where she can max out her 401(k) and even take advantage of savings in the market that are beyond what the 401(k) allows. During that time, she will have ridden two bubbles and two subsequent busts, the second of the two nearly bringing down the entire US economy. On January 1, 2016, this now 60-year-old woman has earned only about 2.15% (based on the S&P performance from January 1, 2000, to December 31, 2015).

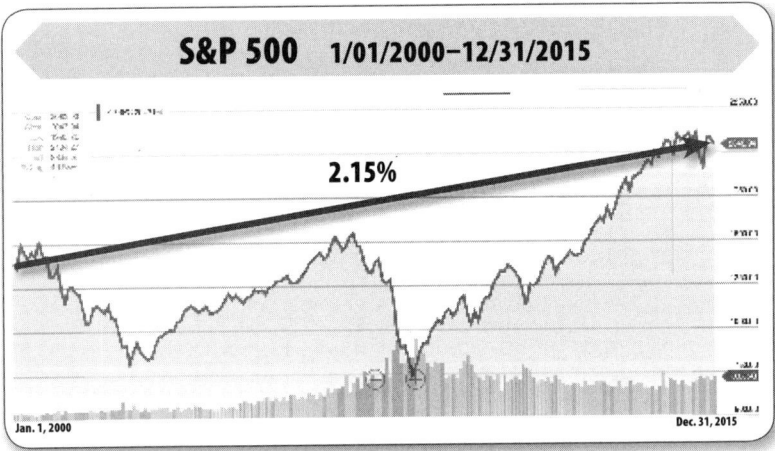

FIGURE 2.1. *So much for consistently earning 8%–10% annual returns by investing in the stock market. The S&P 500 increased just 2.15% annually during the 16 years from January 1, 2000, to December 31, 2015. Source: Yahoo Finance.*

Her window was 16 years. She was told to buy and hold, which she did. She is closer to retirement, and her appetite for risk has most certainly waned. If she even has the patience to continue to hang in there, she certainly is losing sleep when she considers daily that the market has never in its history seen the continual growth that it has currently experienced. Anxious. That is the adjective that best describes this woman, and it is believing in the status quo that led her straight into this state.

Averages Don't Mean a Thing

Risk. That is what we are focusing on here. Your 401(k) and IRA certainly have the potential for huge upsides, but they come at the price of accepting probably more risk than you'd like. More importantly, the approach is one of timing, and as in that last example in the previous section, our fictional 45-year-old woman who finally maxed out her 401(k) was unfortunate enough to do so when the next 16 years of the market would deliver less than 3%.

Think about that just for a minute. Three percent! This gal worked hard her whole life, probably did all she could to sock away what she could as she raised her children, developed a career, established her home, and on and on. What does she get for that hard work? She gets smacked down by the realities of a market that has had a fantastic run since 2009 but over the period that she has invested has delivered an actual return of **less than 3%**.

It's a shame, because that gal, and millions like her, deserves better. Everyone deserves an approach that doesn't insist that he or she just buckle up for the ride because the 80-year track record of the market delivers between 8% and 10%. News flash for you reading this right now: you do not have an 80–90-year investment horizon. Your investment is probably between 5 and 30 years. Why go on about it like that? Because there is one misleading term or phrase used when companies market stock-market-related investments such as the 401(k) and IRA. The term or phrase that needs to be exposed is called "average returns."

Look at it this way. Let's assume the market plummets by 50% in one year but then rallies to deliver a 50% gain the very next year. The average return for those two years would be 0%. Not too terrible when you consider that year 1 was a catastrophe. But the ***actual return*** on the actual money in the actual accounts that were on the roller coaster ride lost money overall—a 25% loss, for that matter. This is a silly simple example, but let's not kid ourselves. The math is simple. If we have a dollar and lose 50 cents, a 50% gain on what we have left doesn't get us back to a dollar, now does it? Of course not, it only gets you back to ¢75. That's it. This is why ***we really shouldn't pay attention to the average returns over any period of the market***. Rather, we should look at the actual performance.

OK, let's move away from the simple and look at a real example over the course of the 21-year period from 1995 through 2015. See Figure 2.2. This period included the five best consecutive years the market ever had, from 1995 through 1999. But it also includes two brutal stock market corrections. If a $10,000 annual contribution is made, you can see that the average yield during this time is calculated at about 9.16%. Not too shabby. That being said, if we look at the actual yield over this same period of time, we see it is a much different story. That actual return comes in at a more modest 5.82%. So much for the 8%–10% actual returns you were told you could expect.

This is the reality of what risk means to us. Unless we can somehow predict the movement of the market and have the ability to constantly manipulate our account distributions, this is what recent history tells us about what we can expect. But market timing is impossible; in fact, most of us move money out of the market well into a bear market and

YEAR	ANNUAL YIELD	AVERAGE RETURN	ACTUAL RETURN	ACTUAL VALUE
1995	34.11%	34.11%	34.11%	13,411
1996	20.26%	27.19%	25.08%	28,154
1997	31.01%	28.46%	27.80%	49,985
1998	26.69%	28.02%	27.40%	75,995
1999	19.51%	26.32%	25.07%	102,773
2000	(10.14%)	20.24%	15.20%	101,338
2001	(13.04%)	15.49%	8.12%	96,819
2002	(23.37%)	10.63%	0.51%	81,856
2003	26.38%	12.38%	5.05%	116,088
2004	8.99%	12.04%	5.71%	137,423
2005	3.00%	11.21%	5.29%	151,846
2006	13.62%	11.42%	6.41%	183,889
2007	4.22%	10.86%	6.13%	202,071
2008	(38.49%)	7.34%	(0.95%)	130,445
2009	23.45%	8.41%	1.79%	173,379
2010	12.78%	8.69%	2.96%	206,815
2011	0.00%	8.18%	2.65%	216,815
2012	13.41%	8.47%	4.05%	257,231
2013	29.60%	9.58%	5.70%	346,331
2014	11.00%	9.65%	6.12%	395,528
2015	(0.73%)	9.16%	5.82%	402,568

FIGURE 2.2. *A $10,000 annual investment in the S&P 500 from 1995 through 2015 delivered a 9.16% average return and a much more modest 5.82% actual return.*

don't put it back in until the bull has been running for a year or so. That compounds the problem here, because any management that we are trying to impose over the risk ends up making matters worse.

The Truth of Tax Deferment

OK, where are we so far on evaluating the 401(k) and IRA? (1) They are risky, (2) buy and hold works great over an 80-plus-year period, but most of you reading this book probably have a 5–30-year investment window, and (3) they are sold on a misleading "average return" that we'll never actually benefit from. What about the tax-deferred benefit? Surely, that has a differentiating value enough for us to assume risk regardless of what our actual return ends up being, doesn't it?

FIGURE 2.3. *The US national debt in excess of $20 Trillion in $100 bills. Courtesy* http://www.demonocracy.info.

I always answer this question with a question of my own that I'll put to you now. Once again, I'd really like you to pause for a moment and honestly and genuinely answer. Here goes.

Do you think taxes will be higher or lower in the future?

I know how you answered because I've asked this question of thousands of people who have attended hundreds of financial workshops that I've conducted over the past 10 years. Everyone, and I mean everyone, answers that question the same way. Actually, everyone answers not only the same way but also **in** the same way. It goes like this. First, people in the audience sort of snort, chuckle, or flat-out laugh out loud. Then they say something along the lines of, "Of course they are going to be higher." Everyone thinks taxes are going to be higher.

The reasons why are pretty obvious, but I really want to hammer home the obvious for a moment because I think it is important to emphasize so that I can underscore a point.

The image in Figure 2.3 is one that you may have seen before.

The large towers that surround the Statue of Liberty represents, in $100 bills, our national debt, which at the time of writing this second edition is almost 22 trillion dollars. A lot of money, no? You bet it is, but it is such a large amount that we can't possibly get our heads around that number. This picture helps puts it into perspective.

Debt means the US government has a bill to pay, and the only means of revenue that the government has at its disposal are taxes, and the truth of the matter is that as I write this second edition in 2018, the marginal tax rate is actually pretty low, historically speaking.

Now, this notion of the marginal tax rate being low is one that I sometimes shudder to bring up at my seminars because many of us feel we are taxed too high already, and sometimes people let me know it when I suggest that the marginal rate is historically low. But I bring it up nonetheless because the current state of the marginal tax rate isn't a political discussion; it is a reality discussion. Let me explain by using the image in Figure 2.4 below:

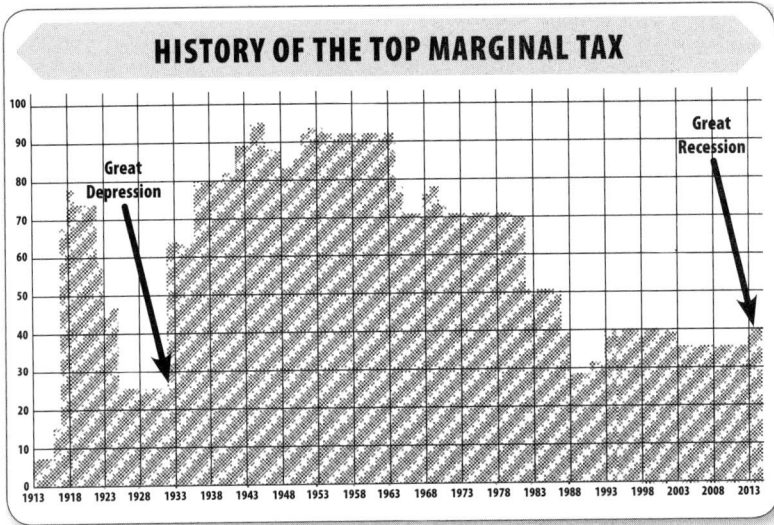

FIGURE 2.4. *Taxes are a bargain today compared to where they have been in the past.*

The idea of a law that guarantees the government revenue is far younger than the country itself. The 16th Amendment, passed in 1913, is what gave the US government the legal authority to tax income. The chart you see here shows you the resulting marginal tax rate that the government has imposed since the IRS was born. There are two things to note here. The first is obvious. Relative to the entire history of taxation in the United States, the current marginal tax rate is fairly low. But the second thing to look at is the period after the Great Depression and World War II, when taxes climbed and were on their way to their height. One major economic event and one major military clash led to higher taxes. Our current national debt is high in part because of the response to the Great Recession and the war on global terrorism, one major economic event and an ongoing military struggle. If you add to this the questionable health of some major government programs such as Social Security, you will quickly understand why you feel in your gut that taxes in the future will be markedly higher. I mean, come on: you don't need an advanced degree in economics to know that to address some of the major issues of our fiscal health, the government is going to need more revenue.

What is the point of all of this? Well, you most likely chuckled to yourself when I asked whether taxes were going higher and probably nodded your head during the discussion of debt and the marginal tax rate. Yet the 401(k) and IRA are financial vehicles that defer your taxes until a later time when you just agreed they would be higher. See where I'm headed with this?

Taxes in our qualified plans aren't avoided; they are deferred. This is not a revelation, of course, and we all know this to be fact, but I can tell you from experience that hardly anyone ever mentally factors in what the bite out of his or her retirement income is going to look like when he or she becomes responsible for paying those taxes. Don't take my word for it, though; I would encourage you to seek out the 70-somethings in your life and ask them how they feel about the income tax that leaves their hands every time they draw on their qualified account. They're not going to be smiling when they tell you the answer, and I promise you that if they are honest, they are going to come clean with you that they really hadn't anticipated how much that tax bill would sting.

There is a cost to deferring your taxes; unfortunately, no one ever examines it in order for us to make a better decision over whether that cost is worth accepting. Let me explain.

Let's assume that a young woman in the 33% tax bracket began saving when she was 35 years old. She puts $4,000 away diligently into an IRA. So her total annual tax deferment will be about $1,320. Now to make it easy, we'll do two things. First, we'll give her an annual return on her investment of 10%. Yeah, I know we just spent time calling out the fact that the market will probably never give you year-over-year actual growth of 10%, but let's just assume that this is what she'll be earning. The second assumption we'll make is that she'll maintain the $4,000-a-year contribution for each of the next 30 years. So it looks like this.

Annual savings:	$ 4,000
Duration:	30 years
Tax bracket:	33%
Annual taxes deferred:	$ 1,320
Total saved at 10%:	$723,744
Total taxes deferred:	$ 39,600

Now let's focus on the distribution of her IRA. Will she likely take a lump-sum distribution from her IRA? No. Where would she put it? Instead, she will likely withdraw the money over time. Let's assume a 10% withdrawal each year, as she continues to earn 10% on the balance. Believe it or not, I'm trying to make this look as good as I can for her.

Annual withdrawal:	$72,000
Tax bracket:	33%
Annual taxes paid:	$23,760
Net income:	$48,240

The bottom line here is that between the ages of 65 and 85, this woman will have **paid** over $450,000 in taxes for the **right** to have saved $39,600. Please explain the tax efficiency of this approach—please.

Now, one of the first arguments that people make when I run through this example goes something like this: "Yeah, but wait a minute—you've kept her in the same tax bracket. My accountant told me I will be in a lower tax bracket." You see, this right here is why you need a team of advisors, which we'll get to later. When I get that question, and I always get that question, I look at my audience and I say the following: "If you are in a lower tax bracket when you retire, then it means you have FAILED FINANCIALLY!" Who the heck wants a financial plan designed to be in a lower tax bracket when you retire? I don't want to mince words. If you are in a lower tax bracket, it only means one of two things happened: it means you didn't save enough money, or it means the money you saved hasn't performed well—and you don't want either scenario. Doesn't it make sense to have a financial plan designed to be successful so that at retirement you are in a higher tax bracket as a result of your successful financial planning and investing? Of course it does. *Putting a financial plan together assuming that you'll be in a lower tax bracket is another way of you conceding that you are going to be a financial underachiever*. Why would you want to be that person? How about you put a plan together based on your being successful and as a result being in a higher tax bracket? That's a plan based on success. That's what I want. How about you? This book will teach you how to deal with taxes that come with your successful investing, as you will see.

The bottom line is this: if you are banking on taxes being lower when you retire, then you are in for a wake-up call.

So with that in mind, let's go back to that perfect retirement that I had you think of earlier. Remember? House paid off, kids grown, big old qualified retirement accounts? Not looking so perfect now, huh? Our income tax is going to hurt, and because our house is paid off and our kids are grown, the two biggest tax deductions we enjoyed our entire lives are gone when we need them most. And what did you get for this "perfect retirement"? Your money completely tied up and illiquid for 20 or 30 years.

Come on! That is brutal. I mean, how did we get duped into this? I'll tell you how.

Free Pizza and a Retirement Plan

Chances are this is how you ended up in your first 401(k). Early in your career, you were at work one morning and decided to head to the company kitchen to grab a cup of coffee. As you poured your cup, you noticed a sign about a free pizza and salad lunch that afternoon. The lunch was part of your human resources department "employee care" program, and the guest at the lunch that day was a representative from Fidelity. The topic was retirement savings.

You ended up going to grab your free slice, and the Fidelity rep started talking to you about free money, something called a match. He told you how you could seemingly swindle Uncle Sam out of taxes by investing money instead of taking it home. And he goes on and on about how the historical growth on this "401(k)" account, which you had heard of but didn't know a whole lot about, was between 8% and 10%.

He sure seemed like he knew what he was talking about, the pizza was good, and free money, shoot, who wouldn't want that? Besides, the woman from human resources was probably 15 years your senior, and she confirmed that, yup, all this is true and a gracious part of the company's benefits plan. She made it seem as though you'd be foolish not to take advantage of the company match, that it was free money that you would be saying no to. You grabbed one more slice to go after filling out the paperwork to begin your deduction at 5% of your gross salary at the time.

Sound familiar? I can tell you that this story, while a little exaggerated, is how nearly all of my clients describe their initial decision to start investing in their 401(k). It isn't a coincidence; it goes down this way because the financial industry has one goal in mind: get more of your money to manage. After all, if the status quo investment plan is fraught with the sort of land mines that I've been describing, why is it so popular? It is popular because an entire industry has evolved around the mechanics of the traditional stock market investment.

Let's take a look at how that industry works and benefits.

The Best Business Model Ever

Time for another question. Let's assume you owned a small business— oh, I don't know; let's say a restaurant. Suppose that you just wrapped up your best year ever. If I told you that every year following this year, you are now guaranteed to start the New Year off **knowing** that every single customer who had a meal at your restaurant would return the following year, how would you be feeling about your business? Probably pretty good, right?

If this were the case, you would have a very healthy level of recurring revenue. Recurring revenue is the amount of money that former customers are going to spend with you again in the future. It is also the foundation for many business models that we are very familiar with. For example, consider your smartphone. The full retail price for the latest iPhone is between $500 and $800, yet few people actually pay that. They end up getting a $600 phone for almost nothing. Why is this? Because the wireless carrier is happy to subsidize the cost of the phone in exchange for a two-year contract that obligates you to pay $100 per month. More importantly, once the carrier has you as a customer, the odds are you'll remain with it and simply upgrade your phone to the latest version from time to time. Just look at the advertising battle going on between Verizon, AT&T, T-Mobile, and Sprint. They all want your monthly cell phone revenue.

Recurring revenue is key for every business, and there are so many examples all around us. How about television? Look at the recurring revenue battle between DirecTV, Verizon FiOS, and Xfinity with Comcast.

I bet you can think of many more examples. Every month I get coffee shipped to my doorstep for my Keurig coffee maker. That's recurring revenue. How about the gym membership I pay for monthly that I don't use nearly enough? That's recurring revenue. An alarm system was installed in my house for free last year. Why was it free? Because now I am locked into a two-year monthly service contract with the security company. I can go on and on. If you weren't aware of it before, now you are. That is the name of the game for any business: recurring revenue.

Why am I spending so much time on recurring revenue? *Because Wall Street and the financial planning industry in general have the ultimate recurring revenue business model.* Let's take a look.

Your Assets, Their Gain (Even When You Lose)

Remember that the 401(k) was created by exploiting tax code that wasn't originally written for the average employee. Also recall that the 401(k) was born in an age where it was more of an augmentation to the retirement savings status quo and not the cornerstone of the long-term savings plan. But there was money to be made with this new approach, and plenty of financial firms capitalized to make that money theirs.

As I mentioned earlier, according to the Investment Company Institute, Federal Reserve Board, and Department of Labor, as of 2014 there was well over $4.4 trillion tied up in 401(k) accounts. After our discussion about tax deferment, I'm hoping that you start to see this for what it is: a guaranteed annuity for the federal government by way of tax revenue once you start your withdrawals and annual management fees for Wall Street–related firms and their advisors all along the way. These firms and the financial professionals that manage these accounts for their clients are paid on a percentage of the total amount of assets that they have under management.

Fees from advisors alone are usually between 1% and 2%, and the advisor receives his or her payment regardless of how well his or her clients' investments perform. Now, obviously, the advisor wants you to do better, because 1% of a larger number is a much larger payday for him or her. But if you don't do well, the advisor still takes a cut. So think about it. When you make a 401(k) or IRA contribution at the age of 35, you've basically locked up your money for at least 25 years, and as a result, you've locked up a recurring revenue stream for one of Wall Street's many companies and their advisors. You would never sign up for a 25-year contract with your cell phone carrier, would you? So why do you do it with a much more important asset—your retirement nest egg—with some firm on Wall Street? It makes zero sense. The 3% would never do that.

Now do you understand why Vanguard, Fidelity, Merrill Lynch, and dozens of other financial services companies have armies of advisors working for them? They all want possession of your retirement dollars that are locked up till at least age 59 1/2. Please, for your own good, put your "Business 101" hat on. You've been told over and over again by all of these financial expects on TV, on the radio, and in magazines and newspapers that the first thing you should do when it comes to retirement planning is max out a 401(k) or IRA. Next time you hear someone say that maxing out a 401(k) or IRA is the first thing you should do for retirement, I want you to take notice for whom he or she works. I guarantee that person somehow works for a company that makes money as a result of your contributing to a 401(k). And it could be indirectly. How do you think the *Wall Street Journal* makes money? Fidelity, Vanguard, and Merrill Lynch advertise in its pages. How about *Money* and *Fortune* magazines? Wall Street companies advertise there too. Many times *Money* magazine and other publications allow advisors from their advertisers to write articles that help to brainwash you that a 401(k) and IRA are the best places to sock money away for retirement.

"But, wait a minute, Dean; my accountant doesn't work on Wall Street, and he tells me to max out my 401(k) and IRA too." Yeah, I know. But how do you measure your accountant? By how much he lowers your tax bill, that's how. If you contribute to a 401(k) or IRA, you reduce your taxes today and you think your accountant is a genius. For most people, taking a tax deduction today is clearly a penny-wise, pound-foolish strategy. But when you notice how your accountant is just one more advisor who is saying the same thing as your stock broker, who happens to be saying the same thing as the guy on CNBC's *Squawk Box*, and is similar to the article you read in the money section of *USA Today*, you connect the dots and believe that maxing out a 401(k) or IRA must be the best thing for you. Wrong! Go reread this chapter from the beginning and tell me how anything I've written isn't logical.

Remember in the first chapter I took a jab at 529 plans as a way of saving for college? Well, think about it. Everyone knows that the cost of attending so many colleges has increased by 5%–10% a year for the past 10–15 years. With that in mind, I challenge you to find me one 529 college savings plan that has come close to earning those returns. Good luck.

You see, traditional advisors tell you that with a 529 plan you'll get tax-free growth on your money. True, you will. Problem is that for the past 15 years, we've had no market growth! But guess what? Advisors get recurring revenue when you contribute to these plans, so of course they promote them.

How about the jab I took in chapter 1 related to 15-year and biweekly mortgages? Banks like recurring revenue also. When you have a 15-year mortgage, your monthly payment to the bank is larger. So, again, logic this for yourself. By making a larger monthly payment to the bank or mortgage company, you are increasing that company's monthly revenue, which makes that company more liquid, allowing it to be able to lend more money! If the bank is more liquid, who is less liquid? You are. Why would you want that?

Let me be clear. The companies and the advisors that manage your retirement dollars want you to make money. They want you to make a lot of money. I am not insinuating that they are bad people working for corrupt companies. I'm simply saying that Wall Street is the ultimate recurring revenue model and the trillions of dollars that sit in 401(k)s and IRAs employ millions of people around the world and make a lot of people a lot of money, even when you don't. That's why you are bombarded with experts telling you to max out your contributions to these plans.

In early 2009 I was at an industry event, and one of the keynote speakers was going on and on about how great a 2008 he had despite the bottom dropping out. Why was it so great? Because his clients, on average, lost *only 19%* while most consumers were down 25%–40%. Yes, that's right; his clients lost a mere 19%. But guess what? He still got his 1.5% fee, so, really, his clients lost over 20% because they didn't get any protection from the crash by spending 1.5% with him that year.

You see how this is absolutely crazy to me. Name me another industry that will not allow you to somehow recoup your money if you are not happy with a product or service. If you go to a restaurant and the service is awful, a manager will come out and discount your check or pay it outright. If a piece of clothing that you just bought has a hole in it, you take it back to the store. Shoot, a company like Costco takes almost anything back even if you have been using it for a year. But your advisor and the companies that he or she works for in the transaction below in Figure 2.5 get theirs no matter what happens to your money.

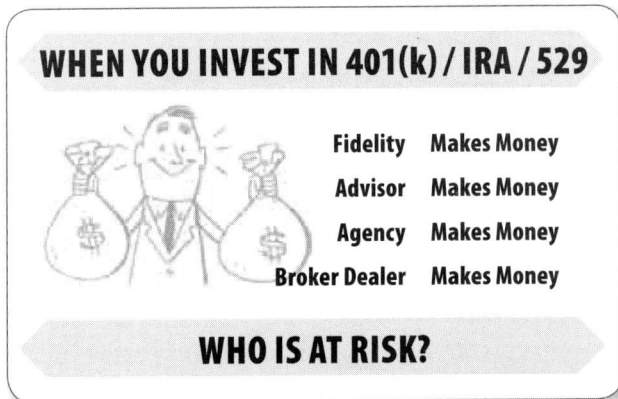

WHEN YOU INVEST IN 401(k) / IRA / 529

Fidelity	Makes Money
Advisor	Makes Money
Agency	Makes Money
Broker Dealer	Makes Money

WHO IS AT RISK?

FIGURE 2.5. *Thousands of companies and their employees generate hundreds of millions of dollars in recurring revenue annually thanks to the 401(k) and IRA industry.*

So are you starting to feel misled? I bet you are. Are you starting to see why maxing out a 401(k) or IRA is for the 97% of the public? This is your hard-earned money we are talking about. I need to make sure. The next chapter will examine the characteristics of the ideal investment. Let's see how your 401(k) or IRA stacks up.

chapter 3

The Ideal Investment

At all of my financial seminars, I stand next to a blank whiteboard with a marker, and I ask my audience to name the characteristics of the ideal investment. I'm not looking for them to shout out the names of specific investments. Instead, I am looking for them to give me the characteristics of the perfect place to save money.

I have asked this question 500 times at 500 different seminars, and I'm telling you that there are five characteristics that come up every single time. Every time!

The five characteristics of the ideal investment that come up every time, in order of importance, are as follows:

1. Safe

2. Good returns

3. Liquid

4. Tax free

5. Low maintenance

OK, take a look at this list above. I'm going to assume that you agree that if you could design the perfect investment vehicle, you would want it to have all five of these characteristics. I need you to nod your head in agreement. Of course you want all of this.

At my seminars, I write these characteristics on the whiteboard, and then I stand back, I turn to the audience, and I ask them two more important questions.

"Does anyone know of an investment vehicle that has all five of these characteristics?" I wait. I wait some more. You can hear a pin drop. Very seldom will anyone suggest something that delivers all five of these characteristics. So now I ask you. Can you think of anything that delivers all five of these ideal characteristics? Before we continue, I need you to make a mental note right now. Can you think of an investment that is safe, has good returns, is liquid, is tax free, and is low maintenance? Don't worry if you can't. Nobody else can either.

Last question for my seminar audience and for you. If such an investment existed, how much money would you put into it? I don't know what you're thinking, but I bet it's similar to what all my seminar audiences have thought. You'd put most of what you have into it. Am I correct? Please say yes. I mean, why wouldn't you? If you've got a hunch that I'll be introducing you to such a financial vehicle in the following chapters, you'd be right! I know, I know; "Too good to be true," you are thinking. I challenge you to stick with me and soldier on until the end of the book. Because I know without question that when you finish, you are not going to have thoughts about the approach being too good to be true; you'll be thinking, "I wish I knew this years ago." So let's take a look at what would make the ideal investment.

Safe

We all want our investments to be safe. We don't want to glance at our smartphones in the morning to see that yet another global crisis or civil unrest is getting ready to wreak havoc on the US stock market. We don't want to constantly be checking our retirement accounts for performance, anxiously evaluating when we need to move our money to a safe harbor to weather the latest storm. No, what we all want is to simply be confident in our choices about where we place our money. We want to rest easy at night with the knowledge that, no matter what is going on in the world, what we've been able to save for our retirement isn't going anywhere, that our long-term nest egg is protected against just about anything and will be there waiting for us when we're ready to use it.

Good Returns

So what is a good return? If I ask 10 different people, I generally get 10 different answers. As I have mentioned, I conduct many financial seminars and talk with literally thousands each year. While this is more anecdotal than scientific, I can share with you that my audience usually agrees that a "good" return is in the ballpark of 6%–9%. Some go lower than that, and some go higher, but, ultimately, I pose this question to my audience: "If you received between 6% and 9% on an investment, would you consider that investment to be successful?" Framed this way, most agree that such a return would in fact be a good one

But this isn't about whom I've asked this of in the past; it is about you. So pose the same question to yourself about what you would consider good. Does 6%–9% qualify as good in your book? I'm going to go out on a limb and suggest that, yes, indeed, if you received 6%–9% on a long-term investment, you would most likely be satisfied with that return.

This "good return" question is important as we move forward, because if you are unsatisfied with a rate of return in this range, then, quite candidly, the remainder of the book might not appeal to you. But I think it does appeal to you; you're just skeptical of something being both safe and good. If that is the case, stick with me!

Liquid

I personally think that a 401(k) or IRA is crazy for another reason I hinted at in the previous chapter, illiquidity. Take yourself back to our discussion about tax deferment also in the previous chapter. Remember that aha moment when I took a look at the cost of tax deferment? Remember that feeling you had when I asked you the question about whether taxes will be higher in the future? Yet we willingly surrender access to our long-term savings in return for access to the funds when taxes will almost certainly be higher and in a period in our lives where we would prefer not to have to pay any taxes.

Why is this a bad deal? Well, again, I'm going to go back to the conversation I have with my seminar audiences. I typically ask whether there is a small-business owner in the room. Inevitably, there are at least one or two. I ask them whether they'd be willing to surrender their businesses' cash to me for the next 30 years so that I could invest it on their behalf. How many business owners do you think raise their hands and say that they would love the opportunity to surrender cash to me in the hopes that I'll be able to get them an 8%–10% return at the end of that time frame? And, oh, by the way, they'll have to pay income tax on any gains when I give it back to them. So guess how many business owners would give me the money from their business checkbook? None! No way.

Even if you don't own your own business, I bet you agree that it would be a stupid question to ask a business owner. After all, business owners understand very well that in order to capitalize on opportunities to grow their business, they are going to need access to cash. And most of these same business owners do not want to incur any debt to fund business opportunity; they want the "free" money of their own cash.

Liquidity matters for the same reason. There are going to be opportunities that arise in your lifetime where the only thing between you and the potential growth of your nest egg is access to cash. Sadly, your retirement accounts and tax-qualified plans are not going to give you access to your own money without incurring some very severe penalties.

Now is a good time to bring up the 3% of people who are financially independent, who we mentioned in chapter 1. I bet you agreed with me when I said that this group of people is doing things differently from the 97% of people who are just getting by. I assure you that locking up money for 20–30 years is not what financially astute people do with their money.

Think of a guy like Donald Trump. When this book first went to print, he was presidential candidate Trump. As I type this second edition, he is in fact our current president. Think for a second about Donald Trump as a businessman and entrepreneur, not as our president. Like him or not, you cannot deny he was an incredibly successful businessman. Do you think this guy made his fortunes by locking up money for long periods of time? Of course not. So why would you? Liquidity allows us all to take advantage of good investment opportunities that arise, and they always do.

Bottom line: we want our money to be liquid because it gives us greater control over how we can map out our financial futures. So most agree that the perfect investment would be liquid.

Tax Free

The Holy Grail: save money, have it grow at a fair rate free from loss, AND allow it to be accessed tax free—not tax deferred, TAX FREE! Boy, wouldn't that be great? Everyone thinks taxes are going higher in the future. So having a financial vehicle that generated tax-free dollars would be a dream come true. Not much else to say on this one.

Low Maintenance

This is another one of those "this is too good to be true" criteria. We are also conditioned to believe that in order to get good returns, we have to be on top of our money almost 24-7. What we want is an investment that doesn't demand we have master's degrees in personal finance. We want the infomercial promise of "set it and forget it."

Look: I'm here to tell you that nearly everyone whom I do business with, have spoken in front of, worked with, or simply traded stories with believes himself or herself to be undereducated on what is seen as the complex issues of investing. We all want simplicity with everything today, and investing is no different.

OK, so in a nutshell, the ideal investment is safe, has good growth, is liquid, generates tax-free dollars, and is low maintenance. As we covered, most people, including most traditional advisors, have no idea where to find such an investment gem. I'm going to tell you where you can, and then I am going to prove it, dispelling every misconception you have ever been told.

But before I get to that, I need to take one more jab at traditional planning—the same planning that you are likely implementing and have been told by all the so-called experts that you should be doing.

Let's compare the 401(k) and IRA to the ideal investment characteristics we outlined above.

Question 1: Is a 401(k) or IRA a safe investment? No, it isn't. Everyone you know likely lost a lot of money in 2008 within a 401(k) or IRA and many others during other times as well—so, no, neither is safe. The 401(k) and IRA fail the safety test.

Question 2: Does a 401(k) or IRA deliver good returns? Well, it depends on what 5-, 10-, 20-, or 30-year period of time you are looking at, as I will prove soon enough. Sometimes it does; sometimes it doesn't. So, for now, let's just say a 401(k) and IRA deliver good returns half the time.

Question 3: Is a 401(k) or IRA a liquid investment? NO! We covered this a few paragraphs ago. Put your money in a vehicle you can't touch for 20–40 years? Crazy. The 401(k) or IRA fails the liquidity test big time. While we are on this topic, I feel compelled to discuss the popular "company match." This is "free money," many suggest, but it isn't really free at all. The cost is illiquidity. Now, look; I get it: a certain percentage of your long-term savings matched is an attractive offer. But I look at it this way. If you are going to give me, say, a 20-cent match for every dollar of mine that I invest in a qualified plan in exchange for eliminating my access to that money for the next 30 years of my life, I'm going to say, "Keep your two dimes, thank you very much."

Question 4: Is the 401(k) or IRA tax free? Nope! Each is tax deferred. There is a big difference between tax free and tax deferred. And I bet you think taxes are going higher in the future.

Question 5: Is the 401(k) or IRA a low-maintenance investment? No, it isn't. All you have to do is remember back to 2008. Were you able to forget about the allocations you had? Probably not. Not that you should be spending hours reallocating your portfolio, but you absolutely can't ignore it. Point is you need to spend time here and there properly rebalancing your 401(k) and IRA portfolio.

The bottom line is this: the 401(k) and IRA are, without question, the number one places that all the experts say you should put retirement dollars first when it comes to saving and putting together a sound financial plan. Yet, if you stop and look at these vehicles and compare them to the ideal place to save money, they fail at least four out of the five ideal investment traits. Eye opening, isn't it?

You want to learn something new about your long-term savings plan, right? You're reading this book because you are hungry for a better way, an alternative, an option that you really want to believe exists. How would you feel about an alternative that is extremely safe, delivers between 6% and 9%, is liquid, can be accessed tax free, and requires almost no maintenance at all? Would that be something that you would want as a piece of your retirement portfolio?

It's time you learned A Better Financial Plan.

chapter 4

The Swiss Army Knife of Financial Planning

Now that we've exposed the pitfalls of the 401(k) and IRA, it's time to teach you how to put together A Better Financial Plan.

The next several chapters are going to tell you about a financial vehicle that if designed properly will do more to improve your finances than any other financial vehicle you can find. Not only will I explain how it works but also I will prove to you, by using redacted annual statements from my clients, that this does everything I say it does. You hold in your hands the keys to increasing your financial safety, rate of return, liquidity, and tax efficiency. You are about to learn how to accomplish this, all with no change in your cash flow, with less risk, and by spending less time managing your finances. If you are working and accumulating wealth, the next few chapters will do all of this for you. You'll see.

For those of you reading who are in your 60s, you're about to learn a financial strategy using this vehicle that will allow you to spend 30%–50% more money during retirement with a lot less fear of outliving your money while substantially reducing your tax liability. I know: too good to be true. That's what all my seminar attendees say, right up until the time that I prove to them how. But before you can learn the golf swing (the strategy), you need to learn about the club (the financial vehicle). So let's start.

How Much out of the Market?

The starting point is to determine how much money you want out of the market. Even though I spent the first three chapters picking on the 401(k), IRA, and stock market in general, I'm not expecting that you take all of your money out of the market. Personally speaking, I have very little money exposed to Wall Street, maybe 10% of my investable assets. You have a percentage in your head. What is it? Is it 10%, 20%, 40%, or more?

Truth is everyone has a number in mind for his or her "safe money," and it is also true that this number changes over the course of one's earning and saving years. Why does the number change? Because the closer we get to retirement, we seek to decrease our risk. We want to keep what we have. There is only one problem with keeping that money out of the market. Less risk typically means what? Yup, less return.

So now revisit the number that is right for you as far as the amount of money you want out of the market. I want you to read ahead considering that number; let's say it is 30%. Realize that if you do nothing else, take what you learn in this book and apply it to some, if not all, of that 30%. Got that? What you are about to learn is going to make plenty of sense for you, but it will be an absolute no-brainer if you consider just the safe part of your portfolio.

What Is It?

We spent the previous chapter talking about the criteria that would make an investment ideal. To refresh your memory, the criteria were as follows: safe from loss, delivers good returns (which we defined as between 6% and 9%), is liquid, can be accessed tax free, and requires absolutely no effort to manage. The financial vehicle that delivers all of this is a properly designed *indexed universal life insurance contract*. *Yes, life insurance!*

Indexed universal life insurance (IUL) is the single most beneficial tool that, when designed and used properly, will combat all of the ills that we went through in the preceding chapters. IUL CANNOT be lumped in with whole life insurance, traditional universal life insurance, or variable universal life insurance. In addition, it CANNOT be confused with an indexed annuity. I have to stress that one again. I am **NOT REFERRING TO AN INDEXED ANNUITY!** The name is similar, but that's about it—kind of like "lightning" and "lightning bug." Annuities have less liquidity than IUL, are less tax efficient, and have a smaller upside. I am stressing this point so much here because there is no shortage of advisors and insurance agents promoting annuities today as a safe haven from the stock market's volatility. Yes, they have some benefits but in my very strong opinion no way near as many benefits as indexed universal life insurance. I just want to be clear on the difference. So do yourself a favor and set aside your inherently preconceived notions about cash-value life insurance. The next few chapters will educate you specifically on how IUL works and prove that when it is properly designed, IUL will do more to improve your finances than anything else you can find.

Understanding Cash-Value Life Insurance in Order to Effectively Use It

In order to understand and appreciate how IUL works and how it is different from other kinds of life insurance, you need to take a few minutes to understand how all forms of life insurance work. I admit that the next couple paragraphs might not contain edge-of-your-seat, suspenseful reading, but it is important that you read the following background information to fully appreciate how life insurance has evolved into the incredible financial vehicle that it is today.

For most of us, the phrase "cash-value life insurance" is synonymous with a product called *whole life insurance*. Whole life insurance is the oldest product that insurance companies sell, and they've been selling it in the United States for more than 200 years. The concept is simple: you pay a premium, and you receive death benefit coverage. Whole life is "cash value" because as you pay premiums, you have a portion of your premiums that the insurance company sets aside as a savings component within the policy. This cash value grows over time and with each premium payment. This is dramatically different from term life insurance, which many Americans hold today and has no cash value. You pay only for the death benefit (more on term insurance a little later).

So if whole life insurance has been around for over 200 years, why does it have such a negative rap? Well, three reasons, in my opinion.

First, for pure short-term death benefit protection, whole life costs a lot more money than term insurance does. So, on the surface, unless you truly understand the tax efficiency and liquidity of the cash value, it appears you are overpaying for the life insurance coverage with whole life.

Second, many view the cash-value component of whole life as too conservative of an investment. Many people think they can get better returns on their own. The fact is that the yields on the cash value are not much better than a certificate of deposit. As a long-term option, whole life won't perform much better than more traditional safe investments. In addition to the conservative yields that the cash value of whole life earns, the insurance company generally pays a dividend each year, which adds to the cash value's balance. It is important to note that the IRS considers this annual dividend a refund on the premiums that the policyholder has overpaid. To simplify this "return on premium" concept, consider it this way: at the end of the year, the insurance company performs either better or worse than it would have liked based on its revenues and expenses. If it performs better than expected, it rewards the whole life policyholders with a dividend that increases the balance of their cash value within the policy. To be fair, it is a little more complicated than that, but you get the idea.

The third reason for whole life's negative perception is what happened in 1979. The Federal Trade Commission practically sealed the historic fate of consumer perception of whole life insurance when in July of 1979 it released the findings of an investigation on behalf of "small savers" who were leveraging "ordinary life insurance" (i.e., whole life) as a

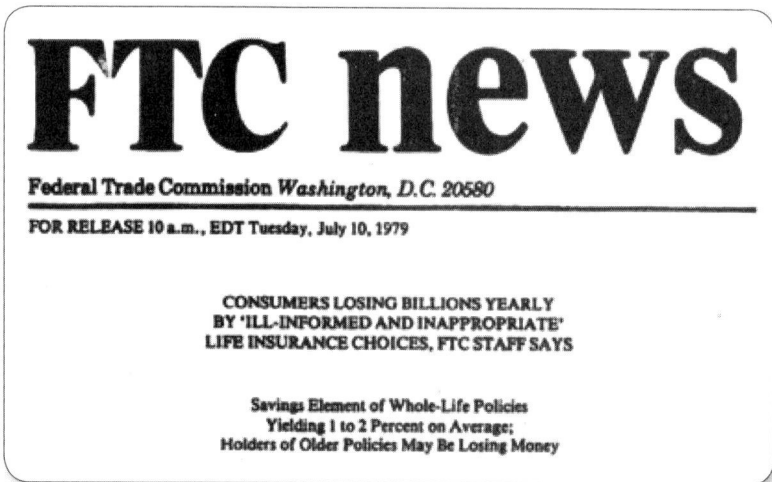

FTC news

Federal Trade Commission *Washington, D.C. 20580*

FOR RELEASE 10 a.m., EDT Tuesday, July 10, 1979

CONSUMERS LOSING BILLIONS YEARLY
BY 'ILL-INFORMED AND INAPPROPRIATE'
LIFE INSURANCE CHOICES, FTC STAFF SAYS

Savings Element of Whole-Life Policies
Yielding 1 to 2 Percent on Average;
Holders of Older Policies May Be Losing Money

FIGURE 4.1. *The Federal Trade Commission's report was a black eye to the insurance industry.*

savings vehicle. The results showed that whole life was performing poorly, delivering rates far worse than normal passbook accounts.

Here is just an example of what the report found:

- Most cash-value policies earn low rates of return.

- Consumers are at great risk of financial loss if policies are canceled in the first few years of the contract.

- Policy cost is difficult, if not impossible, to evaluate.

- Consumers are unable to evaluate cost.

This left the life insurance industry reeling. It was a public relations nightmare that gave a black eye to whole life insurance and left consumers feeling as though these companies were predatory, unconcerned about customers, and chose to shadily keep details hidden from the public. The stigma would last for years and I believe significantly contributes to the negative perception that many still have when discussing cash-value life insurance.

But here is the thing. The life insurance industry is one of the oldest in the United States, and many insurance companies have been around for well over 100 years. In fact, today, life insurance companies are some of the largest and most financially stable companies in the world. What this tells us, and why it is important for our discussion, is that while this terrible black eye damaged the reputation of one of its products, the industry as a whole did not stand still. After all, what successful company ever rests on its laurels? In what industry does innovation just all of a sudden cease, handing the future over to all of the products and services that have already been developed?

None. Not a single industry ever does this. There is always more innovation, there are always new products, and there are always new efforts to please the targeted market. The insurance industry is no exception. The life insurance industry used the FTC report to take an aggressive look at its offerings and, beginning in the early '80s, started innovating its products to better serve its customers. That innovation has not stopped and in fact has accelerated in pace, leading to the introduction of indexed universal life, a product that I believe can radically improve your ability to spend and enjoy more of your money in your retirement years.

Before we get to the details, let's take a look at the product evolution in the life insurance industry since the late '70s. But I want to make an impact with the quick education I'm about to give you, so, once again, let's start with questions. When you think of '80s cell phone technology, what image comes to mind? I think of the famous scene from the 1986 Oliver Stone film *Wall Street*, where Michael Douglas's character, Gordon Gekko, walks a Hamptons beach in his bathrobe while talking on a "brick" cell phone.

The phone represented the gratuitous opulence of the "greed is good" Gekko. The technology was, at the time, not available to the masses. By some accounts, the phone that the factious Gekko holds cost $24,000 in today's dollars. Only the very affluent owned a cell phone. Did the telecommunications industry products stay frozen in 1986? Of course not. In fact, there is a good chance you are reading this book on the latest iPhone or Android.

The life insurance industry has not stood still either. Read that sentence again, because you have to look at this industry as one that works tirelessly to improve the products that it has to offer to its marketplace. It wants consumers to benefit, because happy consumers mean more products. So let's take a look at the metaphorical evolution of the life insurance brick phone to the life insurance smartphone.

Term Insurance

Term gained popularity, not surprisingly, shortly after the dawn of the newly blessed long-term savings plan of the 401(k). Remember that the 401(k) was introduced in the early '80s to augment Social Security and pensions, but once its status was elevated to become the sole outlet for long-term savings, the accompanying story of "buy and hold" to get a reasonably expected 8%–10% return became ingrained in the US personal finance lexicon. The impact on life insurance products was that we were sold on the notion that we would all do better financially if we settled on term insurance earlier in our lives and then took the difference between what term insurance costs and what a cash-value life policy (like whole life) would have cost and invested that difference into the market. "Buy term and invest the difference" is practically personal financial advisor dogma.

Term is a very good product for what we expect. We pay a premium, and in exchange we get insurance coverage for the unlikely event of our early departure from this world. But we have to understand that it is disposable; we own it for a specific period of time and then drop it when the cost becomes prohibitive. If we are sticking with our cell phone metaphor, term insurance would be like those "burner" disposable phones that you frequently see in crime dramas. You know the scenes with these phones. The villain menacingly breaks the disposable flip phone after placing a pivotal call that will initiate some various crime. This is term insurance: purposeful and disposable.

But disposability carries cost. Consider the table in Figure 4.2 showing a 46-year-old man purchasing $1 million worth of 20-year renewable-term insurance coverage at preferred rates.

POLICY YEAR	INSURED AGE	ANNUALIZED PREMIUM	TOTAL DEATH BENEFIT
1	46	1,459.56	1,000,000
2	47	1,459.56	1,000,000
3	48	1,459.56	1,000,000
4	49	1,459.56	1,000,000
5	50	1,459.56	1,000,000
6	51	1,459.56	1,000,000
7	52	1,459.56	1,000,000
8	53	1,459.56	1,000,000
9	54	1,459.56	1,000,000
10	55	1,459.56	1,000,000
11	56	1,459.56	1,000,000
12	57	1,459.56	1,000,000
13	58	1,459.56	1,000,000
14	59	1,459.56	1,000,000
15	60	1,459.56	1,000,000
16	61	1,459.56	1,000,000
17	62	1,459.56	1,000,000
18	63	1,459.56	1,000,000
19	64	1,459.56	1,000,000
20	65	1,459.56	1,000,000
21	66	38,892.00	1,000,000

FIGURE 4.2. *Most people never see how expensive term insurance becomes as they get into their 60s and 70s. Most people lapse their policies as a result.*

His annual premiums will be $1,459.56. On the surface, this appears to be the way to go. Look, however, at the cost of this policy in year 21 (see Figure 4.2). It will cost $38,892 FOR ONE YEAR for this $1 million of coverage if this man decides to keep the policy. Due to this 2,675% increase in premium, this man will most likely cancel the term insurance.

So at age 66, the man in this example no longer has life insurance, and the industry has told him he won't need it because all his long-term investments have done so well over the course of his earning years. But we already covered the fallacies and flaws inherent in that assumption. Besides, his kids are likely grown and out of the house. Again, why keep the coverage? So we assume the coverage is lapsed. And as a result, the insurance company makes out because it collected $1,459 annually from this man for the past 20 years and the death benefit is never paid. In fact, it is estimated that only one in 2,000 term policies pays out. Term insurance is a cash cow for the insurance industry. For you, the consumer, however, term insurance is statistically a waste of money because you will likely die long after you lapse the term coverage.

Look: I'm not at all suggesting not to use term life insurance. I own some myself, and I absolutely think it has its place. But sometimes we need more than a disposable product. And, sadly, this dogma of "buy term and invest the difference" in the financial planning industry is a somewhat misleading and glib marketing tactic that makes term insurance seem like a no-brainer.

In reality, however, the approach is not easily applied. First, very few actually do the math to determine what "investing the difference" means. They simply buy their term life insurance policy and then do what they always did with their tax-qualified plan. In other words, their total amount invested in a retirement plan does not increase by the difference of what they think they saved in foregoing cash-value insurance. And even if they calculate the math correctly, they use the wrong equation. The cost of alternative products is not an apples-to-apples comparison. The cost must be factored against all elements of the status quo. What are early-withdrawal penalties for the "invest the difference" qualified plans? How should volatility be factored in, and so on? It is not rocket science, but it isn't a simple 1 + 1 = 2, either. I'm here to tell you that while, yes, term insurance is a good product, very few people actually "buy term and invest the difference."

Understanding Tax Benefits of Cash-Value Life Insurance

I'm going to get into permanent, or cash-value, life insurance now, but before we do, it is absolutely critical that you understand the inherent tax benefits of cash-value life insurance. If you want to dive into the details here, I would point you to section 7702 of the Internal Revenue Tax Code. You will be able to read for yourself that the proceeds from a life insurance death benefit are income tax free. In that section, you will also find some very specific details about what criteria are used to properly qualify insurance as insurance. The criteria are detailed because monies taken from cash-value life insurance policies are not subjected to federal income tax or capital gains tax, so long as they are taken as a policy loan, which would reduce the death benefit if the loan is outstanding at the time of death. Because this money is not subjected to federal income tax or capital gains tax, the IRS has gone to great lengths to properly define the boundaries of what can be considered life insurance and what cannot. Why? Well, think about it; the IRS wants to make sure it increases revenue to the federal government, and it would face steep opposition from the insurance industry lobbyist if it tried to change the tax treatment of life insurance. So the IRS does as much as it can to limit the use of life insurance as a way to avoid income and capital gains taxes. Another item for you to mentally bookmark and keep in mind, because I'll spend time later talking about it, is how to structure an IUL contract so that the policyholder can maximize his or her expected return while at the same time ensuring that he or she avoids *all* income and capital gains taxes.

There are two important elements here. The first is tax efficiency of a death benefit and the policy cash values. The second is that insurance contracts have to be structured properly in order to have them be qualified as insurance, thus allowing the policyholder to take advantage of the tax benefits of these contracts. Now, as with anything, there are details around how this is executed and exceptions that exist, and understanding them is important if you decide to use IUL to improve your cash position in retirement. But, for now, the point is that properly structured cash-value life insurance has very favorable tax treatment (IUL is our favorite by far, and we'll get to it soon).

I want to hammer that point home here because it is critical to both how you understand the benefits of adding IUL to your portfolio and how you ask your financial planner for the product. I'll get into the details a little later, but the benefits of the tax treatment are maximized only if the IUL policy is structured properly.

I'll say it one last time to underscore the point: ***death benefits are free of income tax and capital gains tax, and so is the cash value inside the policy if accessed properly. In addition, in order to maximize these tax-free benefits and simultaneously minimize the costs and fees of life insurance, the policy must be designed properly.***

Whole Life

We covered term insurance; now let's look at permanent, or cash-value, life insurance, starting with whole life. As I mentioned previously, whole life is one of the oldest life insurance products that is offered, and as its name suggests, it is insurance coverage for one's entire, or whole, life. What this means is that the coverage extends beyond the life expectancy of the policyholder, which is typically defined as 100 years old in most whole life policies today—though, recently, contracts are being written to use 120 years of age as the policy duration.

Now, there is plenty of detailed information on whole life, but I want to just give you a basic understanding of how it works. I'm not looking to make you an expert on whole life; I just want you to understand conceptually what the product is all about.

Whole life has two important numbers that we should be aware of. The first is the death benefit. This is the amount of insurance protection for one's life that the insurance company guarantees in the event of the policyholder's death. The next figure is the cash value. As premiums are paid, the policy's cash value accumulates. The way the contract functions is that premiums are, in essence, covering mortality costs (the death benefit), expenses to maintain the policy, and the savings account. The cash value and death benefits of whole life contracts are guaranteed by the insurance company, and the premiums are level, meaning they don't change over the life of the policy. This makes these policies fairly inflexible, which means that the premiums can not be adjusted that easily, nor can the death benefit or cash value be adjusted. Again, there are exceptions, but for our purposes we should look at whole life as an inflexible option that, once enforced, remains unchanged for the life of the contract.

One more important fact about whole life: it is classified as a "nondisclosed" insurance product. That means that when your annual statement comes from the insurance company, the annual insurance costs are not listed, nor are any other fees. In addition, you have no clear-cut explanation as to what caused the cash value to increase, hence the term "nondisclosed." Frankly, in my opinion, whole life is a big leap of faith that the whole life policy will grow as projected when you bought the policy. But, in fairness to the insurance company, it generally does. In keeping with our cell phone metaphor, we're still talking brick phone here. The first of its kind but, compared to today's offerings, it has much to be desired.

Like I said, the industry didn't stand still, so let's take a look at the next step in the life insurance evolutionary process.

Universal Life Insurance

Remember the big black eye that I wrote about a little earlier in this chapter? Well, what do you think the insurance companies did when they picked themselves off the floor after the FTC's report on the poor performance of whole life? They created a new product called universal life.

Universal life has the same basic structure of whole life in that there is a coverage component and a cash value component. But in the early '80s, when universal life (UL) was released, it was viewed as an improvement on whole life for several reasons. First of all, UL was the first "fully disclosed" form of cash-value life insurance. When the annual UL statement came to you each year, it now provided a breakdown of every single fee and expense charge. You also were able to calculate exactly why your cash value went up or down from year to year. I hope you agree that full disclosure is better than nondisclosure.

Another difference with universal life is how the cash value grows. In short, the cash-value growth is interest rate sensitive. When a dollar is contributed to UL, the first thing that happens is all of the fees and mortality expenses come out, and then the balance earns whatever interest rate was declared at the start of the previous policy anniversary date. During most of the '80s, interest rates were in the double digits, so the cash value grew between 12% and 16%. With no taxes! Pretty good? No, really good!

Before I continue, let me make sure you are clear on something. A couple sentences back I said that the first thing that happens with every dollar contributed to universal life is that various mortality expenses and other miscellaneous charges are deducted. The exact charges are determined by the risk class the insured is given after medical underwriting and other declared expenses by the particular insurance company. For this example, let's ballpark it and estimate that every dollar is reduced to

85 cents before the interest rate is credited. Most consumers come to the initial conclusion that 15% for fees right out of the gate is excessive. And traditional "put all your money in the market" advisors are quick to point that out if given the opportunity. But let me make a point as firm and as confident as I can.

In fact, the next two sentences you read might be as important as any point I am trying to make in this entire book. The high fees associated with cash-value life insurance are significantly less than what you will pay in taxes over the life of just about any other long-term savings vehicle you can think of! If there was ever a penny-wise, pound-foolish financial way of thinking, it is that cash-value life insurance costs and fees are too high.

They are indeed high if you compare them to the fees associated with a mutual fund and the advisors who sell them. To make the comparison to mutual fund and advisor fees without factoring in taxes would be a major oversight. It's another classic example of the tortoise and the hare. Cash-value life insurance is the tortoise. Just about any other investment subject to taxes is the hare. And everyone knows the tortoise always wins in the end. I will prove that point to you soon enough. So let me continue.

With UL, $1 becomes 85 cents. But then the 85 cents is credited 12% or whatever the declared interest rate was at the time of policy issue back in the '80s. If you get a calculator out, you can determine that it will take only a few years for the policy's cash value to grow and recoup the insurance costs that were initially deducted. After that, the policy's cash values will compound with no impact from the stock market and without taxes. All you need to do is get over the fact that this is a "bad investment" for the first five years. I'm not sure about you, but I'd gladly sign up for five years to break even if the next 10, 20, 30, or 40 years are going to be great. I hope you would too.

During the '80s, UL made sense, performed, and sold great. So if we are staying with our mobile phone comparison, we should think of UL like the mid-'90s flip phone.

It is a fair comparison, I think, because these phones were very popular, sold well, and helped make mobile telecommunications accessible to the masses. UL had a similar impact on its marketplace.

Variable Life Insurance

So, UL sold great, but what happened to interest rates in the '90s? They began to drop. At the same time, the stock market really picked up steam, leaving life insurance companies in danger of selling only products that did not keep pace with market growth. The response in the early '90s was to create a new product called variable life insurance (VUL). Once again, the basic premise of VUL is similar to both universal life and whole life; there is a death benefit and a cash value. The difference is that the cash value of VUL is connected not to interest rates or fiscal performance of the life insurance company but instead to the stock market. The chassis of VUL is similar to UL.

Let's stay with the 15% that was deducted for insurance costs, leaving 85 cents from every dollar. With VUL, however, the policyholder is given a choice of 15–30 mutual funds to have the cash value's growth be linked to. On the surface, this product made a ton of sense in the '90s. Why? Because every mutual fund out there was growing at a rate of 15%–30% a year. Remember? And how long did all of us think that these phenomenal market returns would last? We all thought it would last forever, including me. VUL sold like hotcakes, until the year 2000 rolled around and then 2001 and 2002. The stock market had double-digit losses in each of these years, and the cash value inside of VUL got crushed along the way.

I don't want to mince any words as far as how I feel about VUL. I don't like it, not even a little bit. Why? Because life insurance should be a pillar of strength in your financial plan. How can something be a pillar of strength if it can lose money like VUL can? If you want to invest utilizing the stock market, go right ahead. Just don't do it risking the cash value and death benefit of your life insurance policy.

Also, it is important to understand that if you speak about life insurance to a traditional market-oriented advisor, one who gets paid a percentage of the assets he or she has under management, he or she will almost certainly point you in the direction of either term (and encourage you to "invest the difference") or variable life. In both cases, the amount of money that you end up placing in the market is a calculable part of the advisor's total asset portfolio. In other words, the advisor gets paid on those assets of yours that he or she helps you put into the market.

So variable was introduced to help life insurance capitalize on positive market growth and eliminate the notion that life insurance is too conservative. If we again look at our cell phone analogy, what we are talking about is the dawn of the texting and mobile e-mail age that ushered in those little black Nokia phones or early BlackBerrys—another evolutionary step in product development from the life insurance industry.

Indexed Universal Life Insurance

Remember that no company (no successful company, anyway) stands still. The insurance companies of the world haven't stood still, either, and they introduced in the early 2000s what I believe is the smartphone of financial products, indexed universal life (IUL). It is IUL that I'm going to talk about from here on out, and it is a ***properly structured*** IUL contract that I think you should consider an important element in your long-term financial plan. I believe the insurance industry nailed it with IUL.

Indexed universal life combines the conservative nature of whole life, the full disclosure of universal life, and the strong upside growth potential of variable life. Combine all of this with section 7702 of the Internal Revenue Code and I believe you have the single best long-term place to accumulate and protect your money. No question about it!

Properly designed, IUL literally changes the manner in which the average investor will use his or her long-term savings in his or her retirement years. How? By tying the cash value of these policies to market indexes without insisting that policyholders take on the inherent risk of the stock market.

This is accomplished by connecting the policy cash value to a selected market index such as the S&P 500 or maybe even a combination of a number of different indexes such as the NASDAQ or Dow Jones. The difference is that these IUL contracts have an index cap and floor. What this means is that the policyholder's cash value will grow against the index up to a contractually specified cap and that the cash value growth will never be below a contractually specified floor.

Let me give you a more concrete example (see Figure 4.3). One policy that many of my clients are currently in is indexed against the S&P 500 with a 13% cap and a 0% floor. So let's revisit the $1 of premium that becomes 85 cents due to insurance-related costs and fees that we've used previously. If the S&P 500 performs well above 13%, the 85 cents earns 13%. If the S&P 500 earns 7%, then the 85 cents increases by 7%. But on the flip side, if the S&P 500 has a bad year and loses 38%, as it did in 2008, the cash values are not impacted at all! Yes, that is correct! IUL policyholders **never** see their cash value decline due to a market downturn. Ever. As in it will never happen.

INDEXED UNIVERSAL LIFE INSURANCE

CEILING

"CAP" • Use of index such as S&P 500

13% • Principal guaranteed against stock market declines

0% • Section 7702 IRC allows for income tax–free growth of cash value and access to the cash via policy loans

FLOOR

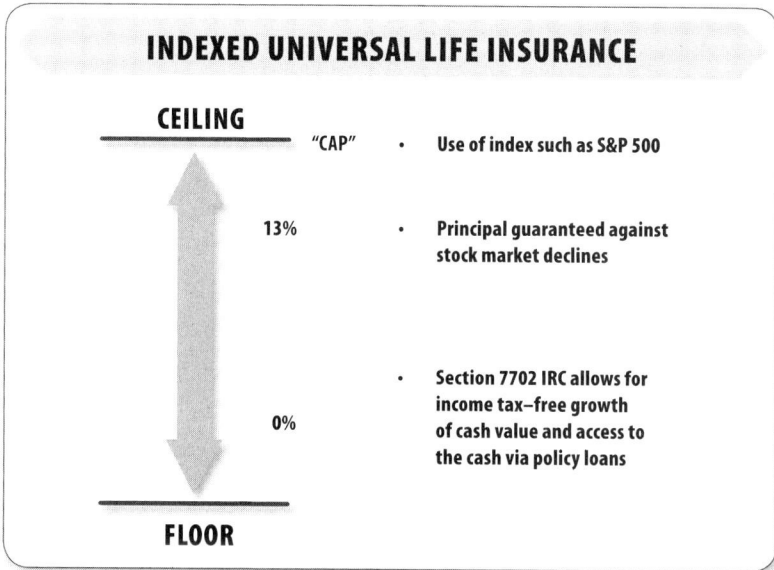

FIGURE 4.3. *The cash value of indexed universal life grows based on an annual cap and floor of an index such as the S&P 500. Most annual caps are between 10% and 14%. The floor is generally 0%–2%.*

Some carriers have IUL with a 12% capped upside and a 2% floor; others have a 14% cap and a 0.25% floor. The important point here is that the policy cash value has the ability to earn some really nice gains, without the downside market risk.

I love indexed universal life. I love the way the product is structured and the flexibility it gives the policy owner.

Remember in the beginning I told you that this book was based on facts, not opinions? Well, the next several chapters are full of proof that IUL works as advertised. I've been positioning IUL into my clients' portfolios since 2004, not long after several insurance companies released it. Candidly, back then I sold this product based on a hunch it would work. But today, more than a decade later, I'm here to tell you the jury is in. Thousands of my clients have purchased this product from me since 2004, and it has performed as promised. They were shielded from the market crash of 2008 and have ridden the market gains since then. I'm going to use a few of my clients' annual statements as examples of proof that IUL works and why the smartphone of financial products should make up 25%–50% of your portfolio.

chapter 5

Lifting the Hood

OK, I want to get into the specifics now, and I'm going to do something that I guarantee very few advisors would ever do: put in writing exactly what sort of performance you can expect to receive by adding IUL to your long-term plan. I'll reinforce these expectations by providing you with some concrete examples that illustrate how a properly structured IUL policy will deliver on those expectations. At the end of all of the examples and details, I will illustrate exactly why IUL meets the criteria that would make an investment ideal. You are about to discover why IUL is safe, why it is liquid, and how it delivers growth tax free, and you will see for yourself the fair returns that IUL delivers. Last, and maybe best of all, you will discover why IUL will be the single best asset in your portfolio that you will never have to manage and will never have to worry about.

Lock in and Reset

I mentioned in the previous chapter that IUL contracts carry a ceiling and a floor that govern how much your cash value will earn. There are no IUL products available at the time of this publication that set their floor with a negative number. In fact, the lowest I am aware of as far as the floor is concerned is 0%. What that means is that the cash value of the IUL contract will never lose money due to market declines, ever. As far as actual positive growth, the ceiling is set at a point that caps growth against whatever index is associated with the contract. Again, to be more specific, if an IUL policy is indexed against the S&P 500, then the cash value gains all of the annual growth of the S&P 500 up to the policy's contractual ceiling amount.

For the purpose of our continued discussion, I am going to use an IUL ceiling (or cap) of 13% and a floor of 0%. So the cash value never grows higher than 13%, and the cash value will never incur negative growth due to stock market volatility. Guess what? This is the first part of our "perfect investment" criteria. SAFE. IUL is a safe place to put long-term savings, and it is contractually guaranteed never to deliver a return lower than the policy floor.

Stop.

Go back.

Read that again.

And in case you resist that forceful suggestion, here it is again in black and white: *IUL is contractually guaranteed never to deliver a return on the policy's cash value lower than the floor.*

This sort of behavior has a name; the insurance industry calls it "lock and reset." In other words, when the index that the policy is aligned with begins to move negatively, the policy locks in at the floor rate. And when the index begins to move positively, the cash value of the policy "resets," or moves with the positive moment of the policy. I'm a visual learner, so it makes more sense to me if I see what the words actually look like. If you're the same way, then consider this image below. This is a representation of how lock and reset works.

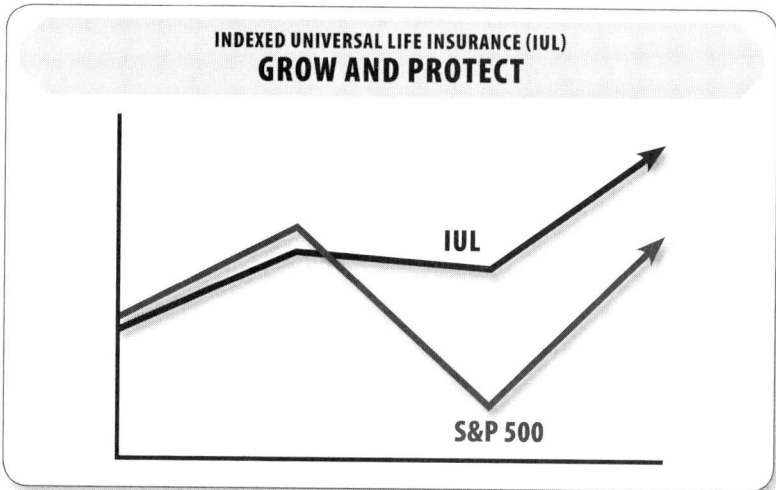

FIGURE 5.1. *When an index such as the S&P 500 declines, the cash value within an indexed universal life policy does not lose money, except for the annual policy fees.*

In the example shown in Figure 5.1, if the policy was indexed against the S&P 500, you will have this kind of movement. In the first segment of the two graph lines, the policyholder participates in all of the gains of the associated index up to the contractually specified policy cap. Then, in the next segment of the graph, as the S&P 500 begins to decline, the cash value becomes locked in at the policy floor. And, then, finally, in the last segment of the graph, when the S&P begins to run positively again, the policy's cash-value growth tracks with that positive movement.

Simply put: the cash value of the policy, in the case of our 13%–0% example, earns all of the S&P 500 growth up to 13% and never loses any money when the S&P 500 has negative performance.

One Important Note

I had a decision to make when I built that image—to make it a general representation of the way lock and reset works or to be as literal as possible. I chose the latter. I tell you that because if you look closely, you will see that the IUL line declines slightly in the middle segment when the S&P is running negative. Why is this? Well, we have to remember that we are talking about an asset here, not an investment, and the asset has value that we pay to receive. That value, in the case of IUL, is not only the cash value but also the insurance coverage. Now, look: I'm going to get into a fair amount of detail about the cost of the asset in just a bit, and, truthfully, I'd almost like to make that line flat just to avoid getting into that issue up front here. But, inevitably, there is always a cynic out there who wants to raise the issue of this expense. Yes, there is an expense, and, yes, the policy cash value will still be burdened with having these expenses deducted monthly regardless of how the index performs. Get hung up on that if you want, but if you do, you risk missing the bigger, and much more valuable, picture here. I will absolutely address this, and I am certain that you will appreciate the explanation. But, for now, make it easy on yourself and just understand that the policy cash value grows up to the indexed cap and will never follow the indexed declines lower than the 0% or whatever floor is contractually stated on the policy.

The Impact of the IUL Lock and Reset

OK, so that is how the lock and reset works, but you can't truly appreciate how powerful it is until you compare the performance of an IUL contract's cash value to how that same money would have performed if it were invested in a mutual fund that directly reflected the S&P 500 performance? We will look at that in just a moment, but at this point, some people ask me why we are using the S&P 500. Well, first, because nearly everyone knows the S&P 500, but I also use that because nearly 75% of all mutual funds available to the average investor *underperform* the S&P 500. So I use it to point out that most mutual funds won't even do as well as the S&P does, and this makes the numbers I'm about to show you even more compelling. I do want to be clear, however, that the index that is used by an IUL policy varies depending on the carrier issuing the policy and, indeed, the preference of the insured.

So for now, let me prove to you how beneficial the lock and reset feature is for your retirement planning. Remember a few chapters back when I stated that the market has plenty of 10-, 20-, 30-, and 40-year periods of time in which it had gains that were a far cry from the 8%–10% returns you were hoping for? Well, let's take a few actual examples and compare that market performance with how you would have done with a floor of 0% and a cap of 13%.

Let's start with looking at how the S&P 500 performed from the 30-year period between 1945 and 1974 (see Figure 5.2). A $1,000 investment made every year would have had an actual return of 4.03%. So much for the 8%–10% you hoped for. If, however, we could go back in time and cap each year's gains at 13% and replace all negative returns with a floor of 0%, the actual yield jumps to a very respectable 6.97%.

In Figure 5.3, we see the S&P 500 performance for the 15 years between 1965 and 1979, again assuming a $1,000 annual contribution.

THE HISTORY OF THE S&P 500
FROM 1945 THROUGH 1974

YEAR	ANNUAL YIELD	YEAR	ANNUAL YIELD
1945	30.72%	1960	(2.97%)
1946	(11.87%)	1961	23.13%
1947	0.00%	1962	(11.81%)
1948	(0.65%)	1963	18.89%
1949	10.26%	1964	12.97%
1950	21.78%	1965	9.06%
1951	16.46%	1966	(13.09%)
1952	11.78%	1967	20.09%
1953	(6.62%)	1968	7.66%
1954	45.02%	1969	(11.36%)
1955	26.40%	1970	0.10%
1956	2.62%	1971	10.79%
1957	(14.31%)	1972	15.63%
1958	38.06%	1973	(17.37%)
1959	8.48%	1974	(29.72%)

AVERAGE YIELD: 7.00%   **ACTUAL YIELD: 4.03%**

IUL WITH 13% CAP AND 0% FLOOR
FROM 1945 THROUGH 1974

YEAR	VARIABLE RATE	YEAR	VARIABLE RATE
1945	13.00%	1960	0%
1946	0%	1961	13.00%
1947	0%	1962	0%
1948	0%	1963	13.00%
1949	10.26%	1964	12.97%
1950	13.00%	1965	9.06%
1951	13.00%	1966	0%
1952	11.78%	1967	13.00%
1953	0%	1968	7.66%
1954	13.00%	1969	0%
1955	13.00%	1970	0.10%
1956	2.62%	1971	10.79%
1957	0%	1972	13.00%
1958	13.00%	1973	0%
1959	8.48%	1974	0%

AVERAGE YIELD: 7.22%   **ACTUAL YIELD: 6.97%**

FIGURE 5.2. *An annual contribution of the same dollar amount in the S&P 500 for the 30-year period between 1945 and 1974 netted out an actual 4.03% return. Had there been a 13% cap and 0% floor, the actual return jumps to 6.97%.*

How did it do? A whopping 1.83%. Not even close to 8%–10%. If we cap the upside at 13% and replace the negatives with 0%, the actual return jumps to 6.10%, a return more than 4% better.

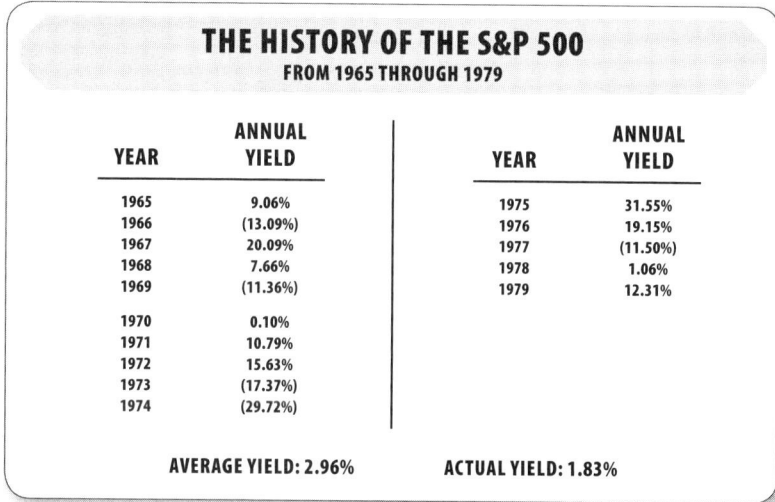

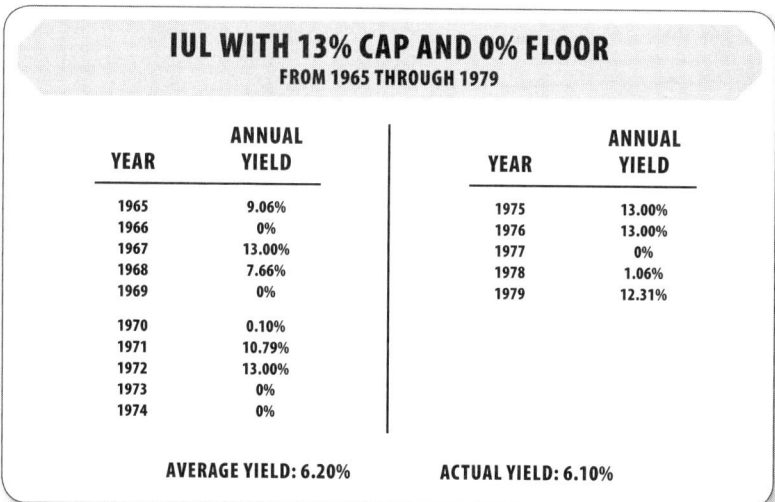

THE HISTORY OF THE S&P 500
FROM 1965 THROUGH 1979

YEAR	ANNUAL YIELD		YEAR	ANNUAL YIELD
1965	9.06%		1975	31.55%
1966	(13.09%)		1976	19.15%
1967	20.09%		1977	(11.50%)
1968	7.66%		1978	1.06%
1969	(11.36%)		1979	12.31%
1970	0.10%			
1971	10.79%			
1972	15.63%			
1973	(17.37%)			
1974	(29.72%)			

AVERAGE YIELD: 2.96%   ACTUAL YIELD: 1.83%

IUL WITH 13% CAP AND 0% FLOOR
FROM 1965 THROUGH 1979

YEAR	ANNUAL YIELD		YEAR	ANNUAL YIELD
1965	9.06%		1975	13.00%
1966	0%		1976	13.00%
1967	13.00%		1977	0%
1968	7.66%		1978	1.06%
1969	0%		1979	12.31%
1970	0.10%			
1971	10.79%			
1972	13.00%			
1973	0%			
1974	0%			

AVERAGE YIELD: 6.20%   ACTUAL YIELD: 6.10%

FIGURE 5.3. *An annual contribution of the same dollar amount in the S&P 500 for the 15-year period between 1965 and 1979 netted out an actual 1.83% return. Had there been a 13% cap and 0% floor, the actual return jumps to 6.10%.*

THE HISTORY OF THE S&P 500
FROM 1994 THROUGH 2013

YEAR	ANNUAL YIELD	YEAR	ANNUAL YIELD
1994	(1.54%)	2004	8.99%
1995	34.11%	2005	3.00%
1996	20.26%	2006	13.62%
1997	31.01%	2007	4.22%
1998	26.69%	2008	(38.49%)
1999	19.51%	2009	23.45%
2000	(10.14%)	2010	12.78%
2001	(13.04%)	2011	0.00%
2002	(23.37%)	2012	13.41%
2003	26.38%	2013	29.60%

AVERAGE YIELD: 9.02%   ACTUAL YIELD: 5.92%

IUL WITH 13% CAP AND 0% FLOOR
FROM 1994 THROUGH 2013

YEAR	ANNUAL YIELD	YEAR	ANNUAL YIELD
1994	0%	2004	8.99%
1995	13.00%	2005	3.00%
1996	13.00%	2006	13.00%
1997	13.00%	2007	4.22%
1998	13.00%	2008	0%
1999	13.00%	2009	13.00%
2000	0%	2010	12.78%
2001	0%	2011	0%
2002	0%	2012	13.00%
2003	13.00%	2013	13.00%

AVERAGE YIELD: 9.02%   ACTUAL YIELD: 7.78%

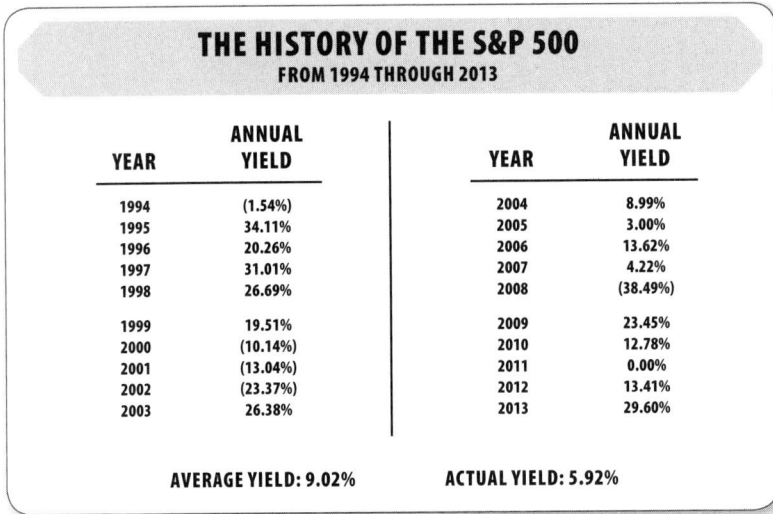

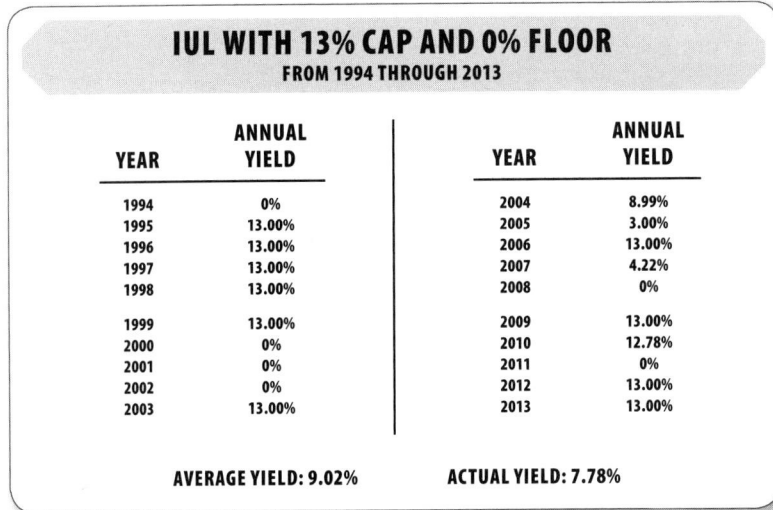

FIGURE 5.4. *An annual contribution of the same dollar amount in the S&P 500 for the 20-year period between 1994 and 2013 netted out an actual 5.92% return. Had there been a 13% cap and 0% floor, the actual return jumps to 7.78%.*

Let's take a look at the 20 years between 1994 and 2013 (see Figure 5.4). The S&P 500 earned 5.92%. This segment of time included the best five years the market ever experienced, during the late '90s. Again, where was the 8%–10% yield you expected? If we cap those 20 years with 13% and provide a 0% floor, the actual yield jumps more than 2% to a very respectable 7.78%.

How about a 40-year segment of the S&P 500 from 1960 to 1999? See Figure 5.5. Aha! Here we go: the S&P 500 earned 9.86%. Fantastic. How would you have done with the 13% cap and 0% floor? You would have earned 8.10%, slightly worse—but still very good.

OK, one more example (see Figure 5.6). How about the 10-year period from 1950 to 1959? The S&P 500 killed it, with a 12.77% return. With the cap and floor, the actual return was only 7.89%.

So what does all this mean? Can you see the few points I am trying to make? Take a look at these five completely random examples again. What do you observe? Well, a couple things. First, the market doesn't always deliver returns of 8%–10% like you've been led to believe that it does over any long period of time. Second, the S&P 500 returns on these five examples range from a low of 1.83% to a high of 12.77%, a pretty wide range, as you would agree. But the returns utilizing a 13% cap and 0% floor range from 6.10% to 8.10%. And if we were together, I'd let you pick any time period you want of at least five years, and you would see for yourself that a 13% cap and a 0% floor deliver you returns between 6.5% and 8.5% the majority of the time.

OK, so now that I showed you a few examples of how a floor and a cap equate to more consistent returns, let me summarize our findings from a much more detailed analysis. The data used for this next set of examples (See Figure 5.7) were taken over 301 twenty-year periods between January 1968 and January 2013. In other words, January 1968 to January 1988

THE HISTORY OF THE S&P 500
FROM 1960 THROUGH 1999

YEAR	ANNUAL YIELD	YEAR	ANNUAL YIELD
1960	(2.97%)	1980	25.77%
1961	23.13%	1981	(9.73%)
1962	(11.81%)	1982	14.76%
1963	18.89%	1983	17.27%
1964	12.97%	1984	1.40%
1965	9.06%	1985	26.33%
1966	(13.09%)	1986	14.62%
1967	20.09%	1987	2.04%
1968	7.66%	1988	12.40%
1969	(11.36%)	1989	27.25%
1970	0.10%	1990	(6.56%)
1971	10.79%	1991	26.30%
1972	15.63%	1992	4.46%
1973	(17.37%)	1993	7.06%
1974	(29.72%)	1994	(1.54%)
1975	31.55%	1995	34.11%
1976	19.15%	1996	20.26%
1977	(11.50%)	1997	31.01%
1978	1.06%	1998	26.69%
1979	12.31%	1999	19.51%

AVERAGE YIELD: 9.45%   **ACTUAL YIELD: 9.86%**

IUL WITH 13% CAP AND 0% FLOOR
FROM 1960 THROUGH 1999

YEAR	ANNUAL YIELD	YEAR	ANNUAL YIELD
1960	0%	1980	13.00%
1961	13.00%	1981	0%
1962	0%	1982	13.00%
1963	13.00%	1983	13.00%
1964	12.97%	1984	1.40%
1965	9.06%	1985	13.00%
1966	0%	1986	13.00%
1967	13.00%	1987	2.04%
1968	7.66%	1988	12.40%
1969	0%	1989	13.00%
1970	0.10%	1990	0%
1971	10.79%	1991	13.00%
1972	13.00%	1992	4.46%
1973	0%	1993	7.06%
1974	0%	1994	0%
1975	13.00%	1995	13.00%
1976	13.00%	1996	13.00%
1977	0%	1997	13.00%
1978	1.06%	1998	13.00%
1979	12.31%	1999	13.00%

AVERAGE YIELD: 7.88%   **ACTUAL YIELD: 8.10%**

FIGURE 5.5. *An annual contribution of the same dollar amount in the S&P 500 for the 40-year period between 1960 and 1999 netted out an actual 9.86% return. Had there been a 13% cap and 0% floor, the actual return falls to a very respectable 8.10%.*

THE HISTORY OF THE S&P 500
FROM 1950 THROUGH 1959

YEAR	ANNUAL YIELD	YEAR	ANNUAL YIELD
1950	21.78%	1955	26.40%
1951	16.46%	1956	2.62%
1952	11.78%	1957	(14.31%)
1953	(6.62%)	1958	38.06%
1954	45.02%	1959	8.48%

AVERAGE YIELD: 14.97%　　　**ACTUAL YIELD: 12.77%**

IUL WITH 13% CAP AND 0% FLOOR
FROM 1950 THROUGH 1959

YEAR	ANNUAL YIELD	YEAR	ANNUAL YIELD
1950	13.00%	1955	13.00%
1951	13.00%	1956	2.62%
1952	11.78%	1957	0%
1953	0%	1958	13.00%
1954	13.00%	1959	8.48%

AVERAGE YIELD: 8.79%　　　**ACTUAL YIELD: 7.89%**

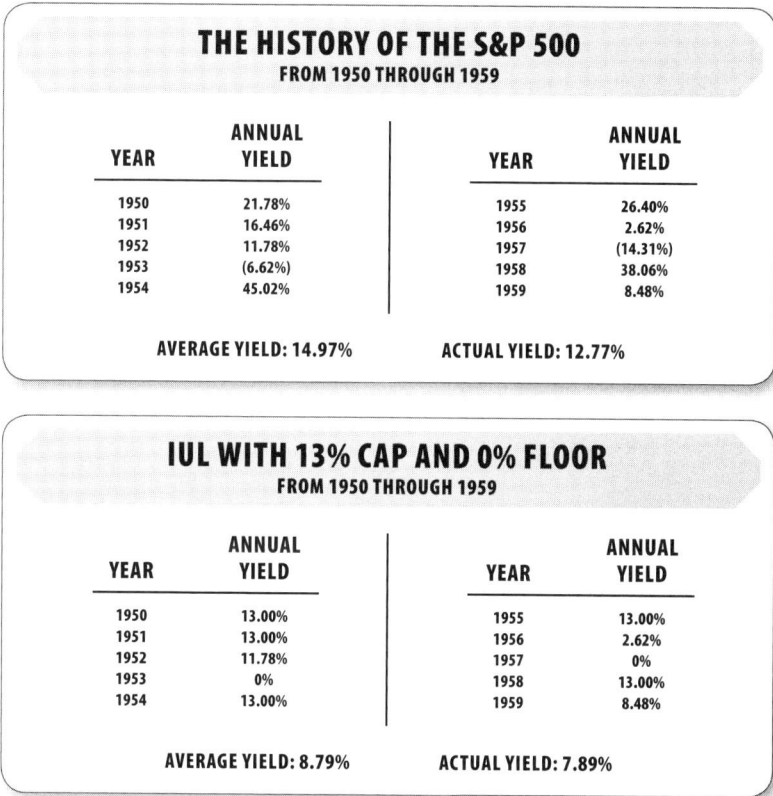

FIGURE 5.6. *An annual contribution of the same dollar amount in the S&P 500 for the 10-year period between 1950 and 1959 netted out an actual 12.77% return. Had there been a 13% cap and 0% floor, the actual return would have been 7.89%.*

is one data point, February 1968 to February 1988 is another data point, etc. The S&P 500 performance was gathered from Yahoo Finance. Each chart, again, shows the *actual return* for S&P's historical performance across that time period and the *probability* of where each of the IUL caps would have performed over that same time period.

We'll start with the high end of S&P growth and look at 8% and 8.5% returns.

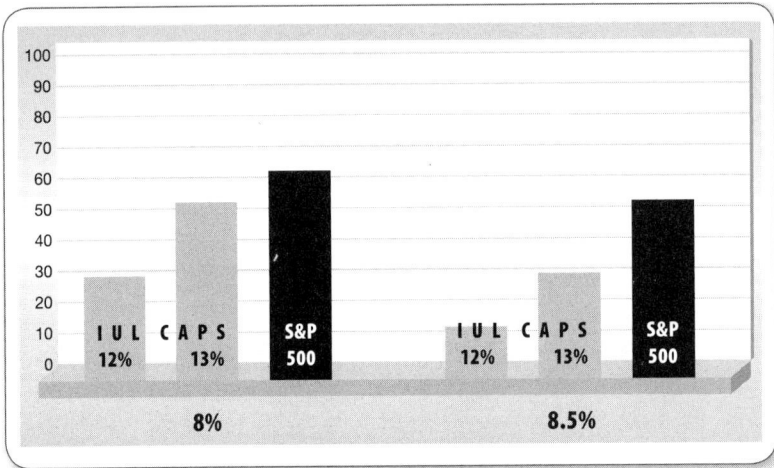

FIGURE 5.7. *Between 1968 and 2013, the S&P 500 was more likely to earn returns between 8% and 8.5% than IUL with a cap of 12% or 13%.*

You can see in Figure 5.7 that the S&P 500, over the course of this period (1968–2013), delivered 8%–8.5% less than 60% of the time. What this means is that investors over those 20 years had a less than 60% chance of earning this sort of return. The IUL, given caps of 12% and 13%, has a lower probability of delivering that return.

How should we interpret this? Well, if you had an IUL policy with these caps, you probably would have done a little better in the market. Not gangbusters, mind you, but you would have had the chance to do a little better. So for the sake of argument, you might earn a half a point to a point more return in the market. But keep in mind you would have done so by carrying significantly more risk than the policy. So right out of the gate here, with the most unfavorable comparison, the decision point is really one of what the investor is willing to trade for safety. Moreover, remember that we are talking safe money here, anyway—the money that you wanted out of the market. I haven't included it here,

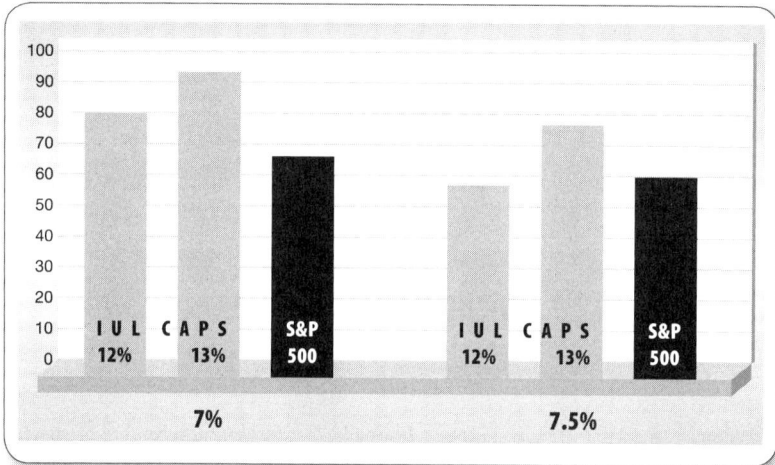

FIGURE 5.8. *Between 1968 and 2013 indexed universal life, with a 12% or 13% cap, was more likely to credit its cash value at least 7% at least 80% of the time. With a 13% cap, IUL would credit cash value 7.5% more than 75% of the time.*

but money markets, CDs, municipal bonds, you name it—all would have done far worse.

But the picture gets better when we take a look at 7% and 7.5% returns.

In this case, the S&P 500 delivered 7%–7.5% at a rate of 65% of the time, give or take. But look at the 12% and 13% IUL policies. The probability that these policies would have delivered ***at least*** 7% was between 80% and 90%! What is more compelling is the fact that even when the return would have fallen below 7%, it rarely falls off by more than half a point or so. In other words, IUL policies with 12% or 13% caps are almost always within 1% of the S&P 500 and outperform 6.5% nearly 80% of the time!

It gets even better the more conservative we want to be with estimating what the likely return of an IUL policy is going to be, given its contract cap.

Let's take a look at 5.5%–6.5% returns on policies that have 11%, 12%, and 13%, respectively (see Figure 5.9).

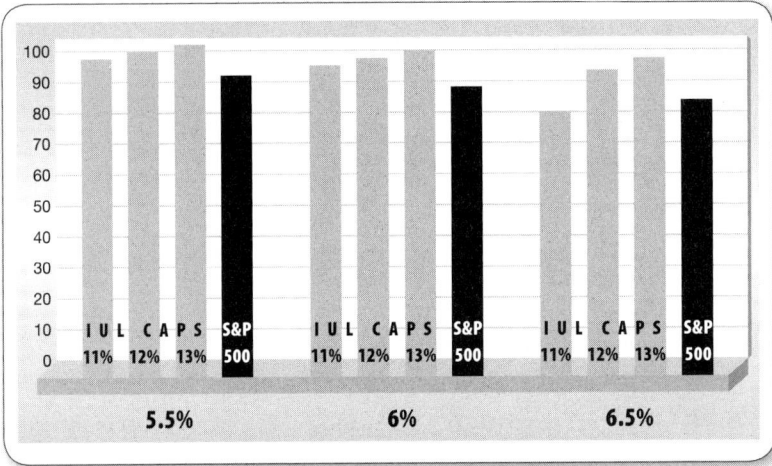

FIGURE 5.9. *Between 1968 and 2013 an IUL policy with an 11%, 12%, or 13% cap would credit its cash value 5.5%–6% more than 90% of the time, and caps of 12% and 13% deliver a credit of 6.5% more than 90% of the time.*

Ninety-five percent of the time, using our historical S&P data, these policies would have delivered at least 5.5%, and, in fact, the 12% and 13% capped policies would have virtually guaranteed at least 5.5%. And, again, we are being ultra conservative with this estimate. I will show you in the next chapter why you have every right to expect more, but I want to use this example to show you that IUL is, in my opinion, the absolutely best option for your safe money—that part of your portfolio that you want to grow at a fair rate but are unwilling to expose to risk.

Second criteria achieved—IUL delivers a fair rate of return! Hopefully, you're nodding your head. But if you want more proof in the so-called pudding, flip to the next chapter. I'm going to show you how this performance works in real life and prove to you that these policies are the best "set it and forget it" option that you could ever add to your long-term portfolio.

chapter 6

Seeing Is Believing

I just want to add a little more color commentary before I dive into what I believe you will find a compelling example. I want to be very clear here. What the IUL policy cap and floor do is very simple. Where the cash value of the policy is concerned, interest is credited against all the gains of the market up to the cap and is protected from all of the losses. Your cash value goes up with the gains but does not go down because of market losses.

To better appreciate this, we need only look back as far as 2008. If you are like most Americans, you cringed every time you looked at your 401(k) or IRA balance in the fall of 2008 and continued doing so through early 2009. You lost plenty, and it hurt; I don't care who you were—the losses were devastating. Now imagine that when the market began cratering in 2008, you had a magic button that literally locked in your cash value at a predetermined emergency floor. Activating that stopgap put a full-on stop for any losses. Let's go further with the fantasy. Imagine that once enacted, your cash balance was guaranteed to absolutely never, no matter what was happening on Wall Street, dip below that floor. But wait! Let's keep going. Imagine now the market is starting to run, like it did in March of 2009, and you want in on that growth. So you hit the magic button again, and, suddenly, your cash value starts moving with the market.

How would you have felt in 2008 if you had had this mythical magic button available to you? My guess is you probably would have felt pretty darn good about the whole thing. And you'd be bragging to your neighbor that you hadn't lost a thing in that cataclysmic financial event.

Well, it ain't magic; it is IUL, and it does ***exactly*** this.

Now, let's look at a very real example that occurred right around that period.

Meet Tom

Tom is a client of mine whom I have been working with since 2005. I am going to use Tom's actual IUL annual statements to illustrate the performance that he received on the cash value of his IUL policy that he added to his portfolio in 2005.

Tom's policy works well for the purpose of our example for a couple of reasons. First, it dispels a myth that cash-value life insurance demands that you pay premiums forever. That is simply not the case with all kinds of universal life if the cash value in the policy is high enough to cover the cost of the insurance. As I mentioned earlier, I will cover the cost of insurance soon enough, but that is not the point of the story, other than to illustrate that Tom didn't pay premiums in the example you are about to walk through.

The second reason this example works well is that because Tom did not contribute to the policy, it is simple to see the way the cash value grew because we don't have to account for the cash-value growth that normally would have been attributed to his monthly premiums. Let's get to it.

August 2008—November 2009

These dates still, to this day, send chills up the spines of most Americans who saw nearly 30% of their long-term-savings portfolios disappear. While the back half of '09 marked the beginning of a modest recovery, the end of '08 and into '09 was a market nightmare.

The policy that Tom holds moves with the S&P 500. So let's take a look at what that index was up to over this time period. As you can see from Yahoo Finance, the S&P 500 was 1,260.31 on August 1, 2008:

PRICES						
Date	Open	High	Low	Close	Volume	Adj Close*
5-Aug-08	$1,254.87	$1,284.88	$1,254.67	$1,284.88	$1,219,310,000	$1,284.88
4-Aug-08	$1,253.27	$1,260.49	$1,247.45	$1,249.01	$4,562,280,000	$1,249.01
1-Aug-08	$1,269.42	$1,270.52	$1,254.54	$1,260.31	$4,684,870,000	$1,260.31

FIGURE 6.1. *On August 1, 2008, the S&P 500 closed at 1,260.31.*

On November 24, 2009, the S&P 500 closed at 1,105.65, a decline of 9.78% from August 1, 2008.

PRICES						
Date	Open	High	Low	Close	Volume	Adj Close*
24-Nov-09	$1,105.83	$1,107.56	$1,097.63	$1,105.65	$3,700,820,000	$1,105.65

FIGURE 6.2. *On August 1, 2008, the S&P 500 closed at 1,260.31.*

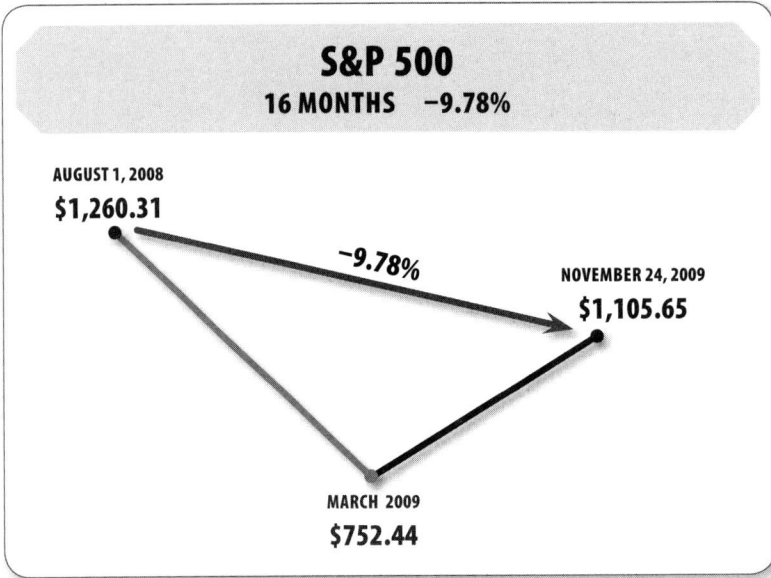

S&P 500
16 MONTHS   −9.78%

AUGUST 1, 2008
$1,260.31

−9.78%

NOVEMBER 24, 2009
$1,105.65

MARCH 2009
$752.44

FIGURE 6.3. *The S&P 500 hit bottom on March 9, 2009, when it fell to 752.44. By the time November 24 arrived, the S&P 500 had recovered to 1,105.65.*

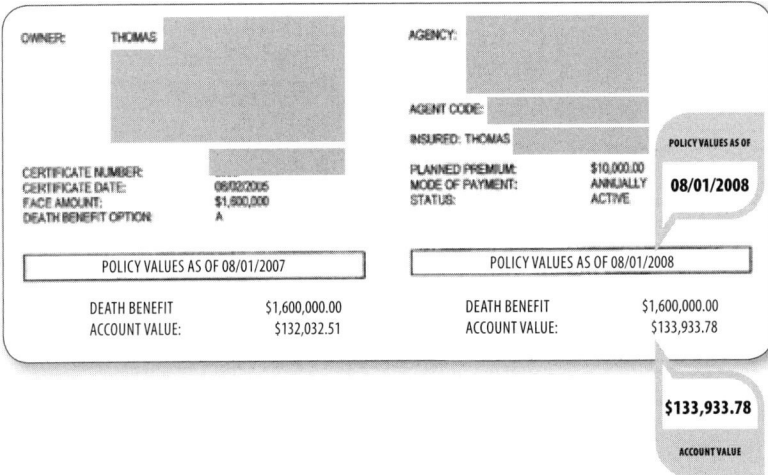

OWNER:	THOMAS		AGENCY:		
			AGENT CODE:		
			INSURED: THOMAS		POLICY VALUES AS OF
CERTIFICATE NUMBER:			PLANNED PREMIUM:	$10,000.00	
CERTIFICATE DATE:	06/02/2005		MODE OF PAYMENT:	ANNUALLY	**08/01/2008**
FACE AMOUNT:	$1,600,000		STATUS:	ACTIVE	
DEATH BENEFIT OPTION:	A				

POLICY VALUES AS OF 08/01/2007		POLICY VALUES AS OF 08/01/2008	
DEATH BENEFIT	$1,600,000.00	DEATH BENEFIT	$1,600,000.00
ACCOUNT VALUE:	$132,032.51	ACCOUNT VALUE:	$133,933.78

$133,933.78
ACCOUNT VALUE

FIGURE 6.4. *Tom's cash value on August 1, 2008, was $133,933.78.*

If you get your financial calculator out, you can determine that during the 16-month time period from August 1, 2008, to November 24, 2009, the S&P 500 dropped 9.78%. I'll explain why I use the date in November in just a minute.

Graphically, it looks like Figure 6.3.

OK, so that is how the S&P 500 performed during that 16-month period. Now on to Tom and what his experience was with his IUL policy.

As you can see from a copy of Tom's IUL statement (see Figure 6.4), in August of '08, he had a cash value of $133,933.

If this $133,933 balance was sitting in a 401(k), IRA, brokerage account, or any other market vehicle, Tom would have had just as many sleepless nights as the rest of the population. In fact, he would have been down $16,437 during this 16-month period.

Original Balance August 2008	S&P 500 Performance	Ending Balance November 2009	Net LOSS
$133,933	−9.78%	$117,496	−$16,437

FIGURE 6.5. If the $133,933 that was in Tom's IUL policy on August 2008 was instead invested in an S&P 500 index fund the value would have dropped to $117,496 by November 2009.

Make sense? It is important that it does before you continue. Tom's $133,933 would have been down 9.78% if his money were invested in the S&P 500 from August 1, 2008, to November 24, 2009. Remember that the S&P 500 outperforms most mutual funds year after year. OK, now table that. Let's continue.

Tom did not contribute a penny to his policy in this 16-month period. Nothing. See Figure 6.6 for the proof showing the section of Tom's statement that proves nothing went into the policy since the previous year.

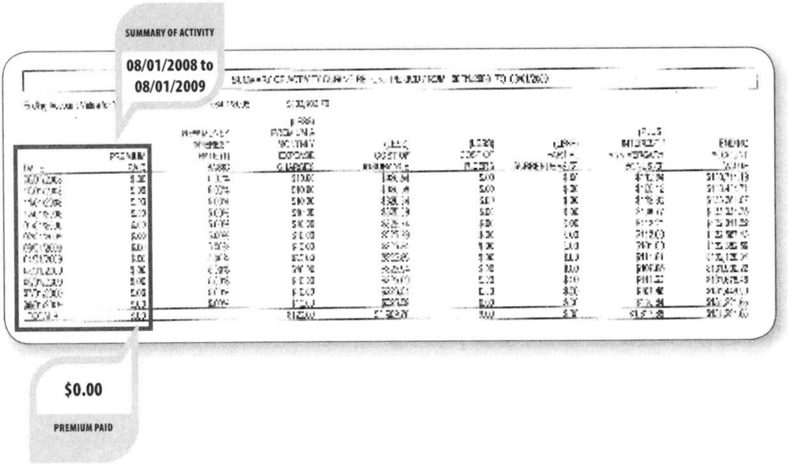

FIGURE 6.6. *No money was put into Tom's policy the following year.*

One year later, August of 2009, Tom's statement looked like this (see Figure 6.7):

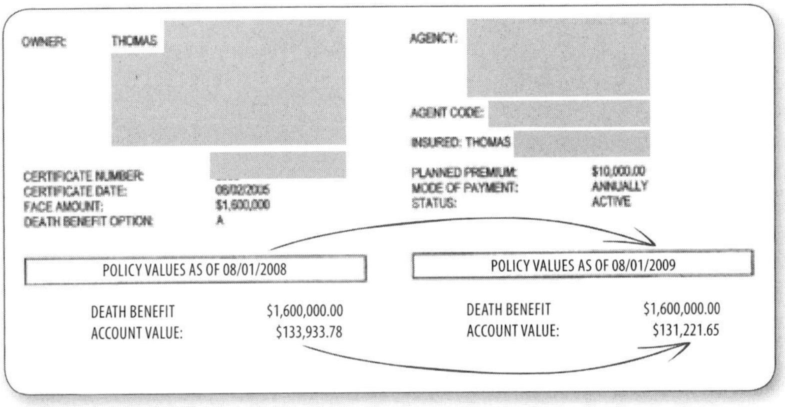

FIGURE 6.7. *The cash value dropped from $133,933 in 2008 to $131,221 on August 1, 2009. This was a result of the annual policy fees and not due to the drop in the S&P 500.*

So his balance actually *does* head a little south. It is now $131,211 and some change. "Wait, what gives?" you might be asking after I've hammered in the fact that the cash value is never subjected to market losses. And that is absolutely true; the cash value on Tom's policy never moved negative because of any market events. So why the slight (just 2%) decline? Because the IUL policy is an asset that holds value and Tom pays for the value that the policy delivers. That value is the death benefit.

We haven't even discussed the death benefit yet (the benefit on this policy happens to be $1.6 million). We'll get to the value of the death benefit a little later on, but, for now, we'll leave it at the fact that the annual cost of the insurance and administration fees accounts for the approximate $2,700 temporary decline in the cash value of the policy. But let's remember what was going on in August of '09; while the market was once again moving positively, *it was gaining nowhere near what it had dropped during the previous year*. Also remember that we're going to end up in November of '09 for this 16-month analysis, and (see Figure 6.5) the S&P performance was nearly a *loss* of 10%. So if we stopped here and suggested that instead of losing 10%, 11%, 12%, or more, you'd limit losses (due to the cost of the value of the IUL as an asset) to 2%, I'm pretty sure most reading this would have made that trade.

Fortunately, it is a *much* better picture than simply limiting losses. Let's continue.

So why do I use the date of November 24, 2009? I remember that date because it was just before Thanksgiving and Tom and I decided to meet up that day to review his policy performance. Shortly before Tom came to my office, I went online to print out an updated copy of his policy value. What I saw was nothing short of awesome. *As you can see from Figure 6.8, Tom's cash value increased to $147,518.93 during the same period in time that the stock market was down almost 10%,* **WITH ZERO CONTRIBUTIONS TO THE POLICY!**

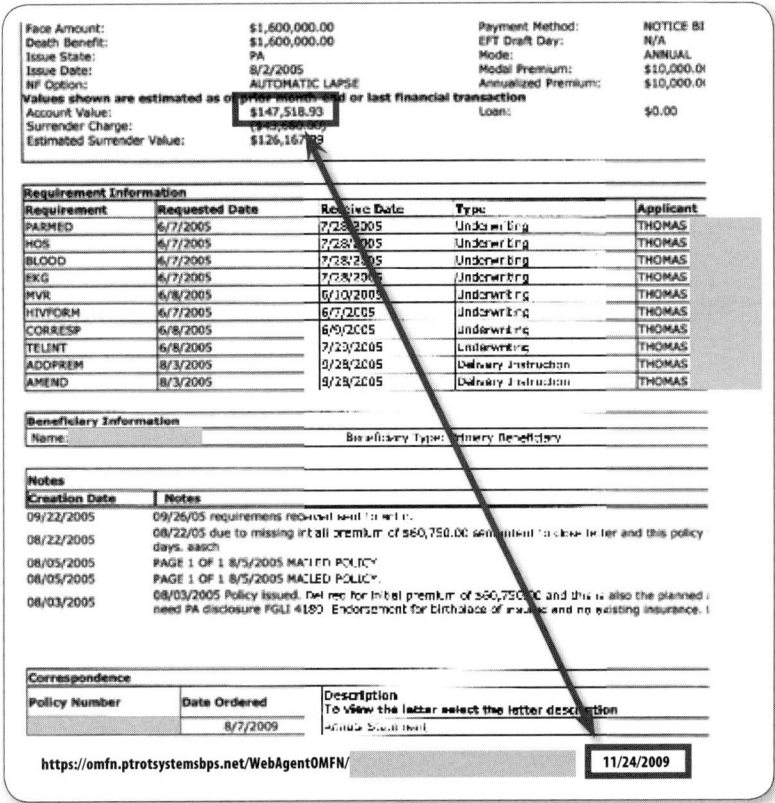

FIGURE 6.8. *My client's IUL policy increased from $133,933 on August 1, 2008, to $147,518 on November 24, 2009. That is a 7.27% increase during the same period in time that the S&P 500 dropped 9.78%. This represents an increase of more than 17%.*

If what you see on this page doesn't make you want to have indexed universal life as 25%–50% of your retirement portfolio, then I give up. Everything you read in the following chapters is going to solidify my point, but this is as compelling as it gets. And this is all you need to show to any other advisor who tells you this is a bad investment.

So let me summarize using Figure 6.9.

TOM'S IUL, AUGUST 2008–NOVEMBER 2009			
Original Balance August 2008	**IUL Performance**	**Ending Balance November 2009**	**Net GAIN**
$133,933	7.27%	$147,518	$13,585
S&P 500, AUGUST 2008–NOVEMBER 2009			
Original Balance August 2008	**S&P 500 Performance**	**Ending Balance November 2009**	**Net LOSS**
$133,933	−9.78%	$117,496	−$16,437

FIGURE 6.9.

You are reading that exactly right. Tom experienced more than a 17% positive swing on the $133,933. Instead of losing $16,000, he *gained* $13,000. And he did it without having to have some magic button that we described earlier. The policy just works this way.

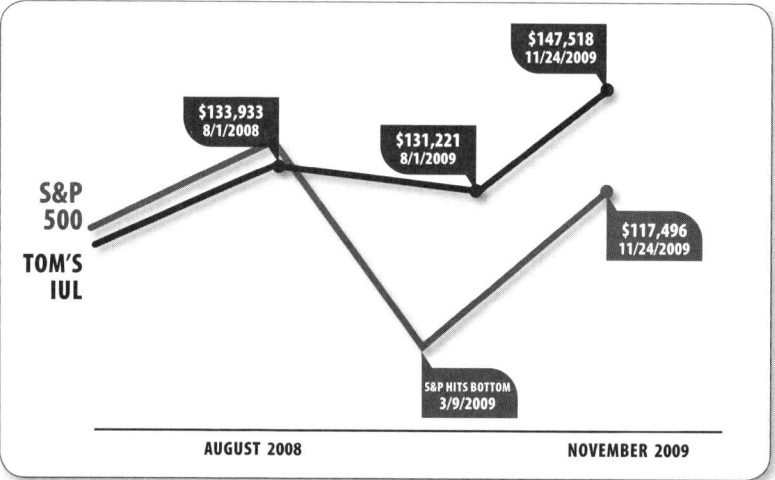

FIGURE 6.10. *The "lock and reset" feature of IUL prevents the cash value from being negatively impacted by market declines. When the market started to run as it did in early 2009, the cash value started to increase as well, except it did so from a much higher starting point.*

83

Visually, Figure 6.10 is representative of what was going on during this 16-month period.

I think it really hammers home the benefit of the long-term portfolio. You can see here that even though Tom is paying for the value in the IUL as an asset in his portfolio, the lock and reset feature of the product performs exactly as advertised, shielding Tom from all of that '08–'09 volatility. The recovery would slowly move forward over the next several years, and Tom received all of the benefit of that growth—with one big difference: when another correction comes, he won't lose any of that forward progress.

Perhaps the best part of the approach? It required Tom to do absolutely nothing when the bottom was falling out in the fall of 2008. Did you have the same carelessness as more and more bad financial news hit headlines that fall? My bet is you made plenty of calls to your advisor or were logging into your accounts almost daily.

Low maintenance—another criteria met by IUL. And just so we are keeping track, here is your IUL "perfect investment" scorecard so far:

- Safe

- Delivers Fair Rate of Return

- Low Maintenance

I use Tom as an example because of the parameters I mentioned earlier that make his case an easy step-by-step walkthrough to demonstrate exactly how the policy performs. While the results in and of themselves should be compelling enough, in my opinion, for anyone to take a hard look at IUL as an alternative option for his or her long-term-savings strategy, understanding how the product works is critical in that decision-making process.

With that in mind, I want to take a closer look at the real cost of the value of the asset, the cost of insurance, and also how valuable IUL is for anyone no matter his or her age. So in our next chapter we'll meet Phil, another client of mine who purchased his IUL policy when he was 61 and at the time of writing this book is now 69.

chapter 7

A No-Brainer
Even at 69

I want to ask you a very simple question. Just mentally note your initial reaction. Ready? OK, here goes.

What immediately comes to mind if I say "permanent life insurance and a 69-year-old man"?

So? What did you come up with? Well, if you are like most of the people whom I speak to, you probably thought things like "doesn't need it" or "too expensive," maybe even "Seriously?" Yes, I am serious: properly structured IUL is an absolute no-brainer for any senior, and in this chapter, I'm going to map out exactly why this is the case. In fact, it is my bet that at the end of the chapter, you will come to the conclusion that, yes, indeed, through the way the case is made, IUL looks like a solid option for a 69-year-old man or woman. Moreover, you will probably come to the conclusion that if it is right for a 69-year-old, then it makes even more sense to add a properly structured IUL policy to the safe part of anyone's portfolio, regardless of age.

OK, let's dive in and shake loose all the perceptions that you have about life insurance's value, value that will far exceed the status quo today of going with a strategy of "buy term life insurance and invest the difference."

Meet Phil

Once again, I want to introduce you to one of my clients, Phil, to make it a little easier to step through the example. Phil and I met when he was 61 years old in 2006, making him 69 in late 2014 when his IUL annual statement was issued that we will be examining shortly. Phil is the poster child for having done everything by the book. He diligently contributed to his 401(k), he had several brokerage accounts with money invested in the market, and he was comfortable putting off his Social Security draw until the full retirement age of 66.

Phil was concerned about the impact that taxes were going to have on his nest egg when it was to become his sole source of income, and he felt as though the real estate bubble of the early 2000s was inevitably going to burst (boy, was he ever right!). He was frustrated, however, with the limited options available to him that would deliver the sort of growth he needed to sustain his lifestyle in retirement. He needed a fair rate of return, more than he could have received from CDs or something similar, but he was unwilling to trade risk for higher growth. Phil, to put it mildly, was a perfect candidate for exploiting the power of a properly structured IUL contract.

There was just one problem. When Phil and I started to take a look at his situation, his first reaction to the idea of permanent life insurance was exactly what we just covered above: too expensive, unnecessary, and I am pretty sure he threw in a very sarcastic "Seriously?" In fact, the week before Phil and I met, he had literally just canceled his term and was increasing the amount he was adding to his mutual funds by that amount. So, to say that Phil was not at all receptive to the idea of leveraging the cash value in an IUL would be an understatement.

How did Phil, a man in his 60s, come to hold an IUL permanent life insurance policy? I walked him through a similar example that you are about to walk through. There is only one difference. The example I walked Phil through was a simulation. What you are about to step through are the *actual results* of Phil's policy that has been in effect since December of 2006.

Phil's Starting Point

Figures 7.1 and 7.2 show snapshots of Phil's statement from which we are going to pull the numbers that make the case for why it made sense for him then and why he is reaping the proposed benefits today.

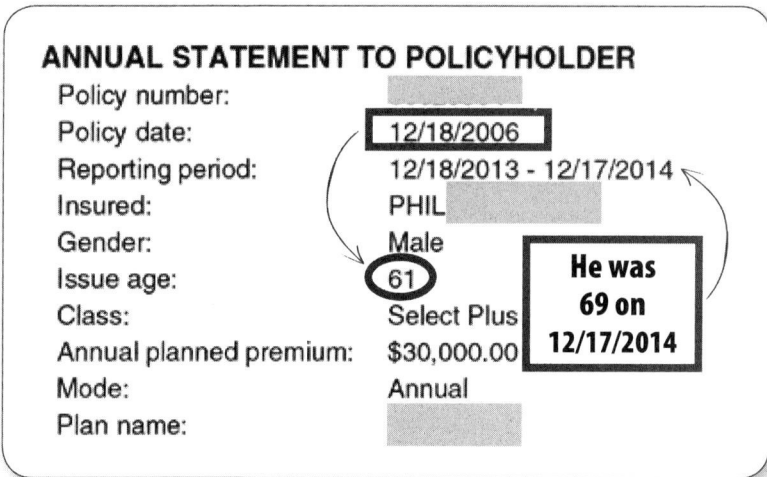

ANNUAL STATEMENT TO POLICYHOLDER

Policy number:
Policy date: 12/18/2006
Reporting period: 12/18/2013 - 12/17/2014
Insured: PHIL
Gender: Male
Issue age: 61
Class: Select Plus
Annual planned premium: $30,000.00
Mode: Annual
Plan name:

He was 69 on 12/17/2014

FIGURE 7.1. *Phil's policy was issued on December 18, 2006. He was 61 years old on that date. He was 69 on December 17, 2014, the date his annual statement was issued that we are using in this example.*

The first thing you see in Figure 7.1 is the section that proves when the policy was issued, Phil's age at the time, and his age at the time this annual statement was delivered on December 17, 2014. The name of the insurance company doesn't matter for this exercise, because most IUL policies in existence from most insurance companies operate similarly to the example you see here.

OK, now to the details. Important point number one: take a look at a section of page 2 of Phil's annual statement. Direct your attention to the death benefit that you see in Figure 7.2.

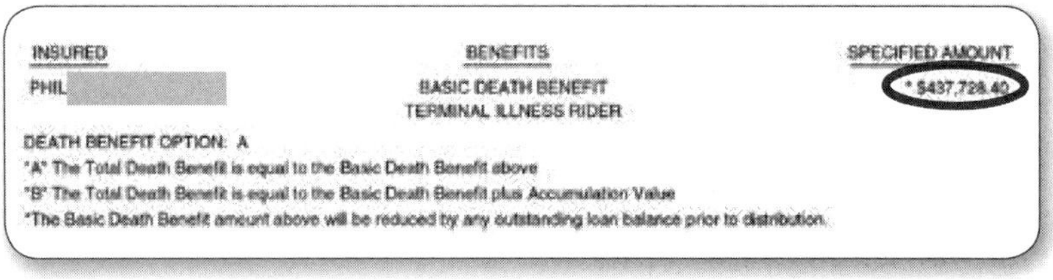

FIGURE 7.2. *Phil's $437,728.40 death benefit represents the smallest death benefit he could have while still enjoying the tax benefits from section 7702 of the Internal Revenue Code.*

The death benefit on Phil's policy is $437,728.40. I want you to read that figure again. In fact, I think I'll type it again on a line all by itself because the point I am about to make is absolutely critical if you want to better understand how to leverage IUL for your long-term retirement plan.

$437,728.40

If you are like most, you are probably puzzled as to why the death benefit is such a randomly specific number. I mean, whoever tells his or her financial advisor or insurance agent that he or she wants coverage down to the penny? So why the odd number, and why the 40 cents? Because it is not at all about the death benefit!

This is not to suggest that the death benefit doesn't matter. It does matter, and it is a difference maker that, as I keep telling you, we'll get to shortly. The reason that the death benefit is so seemingly random and specific is because to maximize the way the cash value in a policy performs, we have to determine, down to the penny, the absolute minimum amount of coverage we can purchase. In the previous chapters, you should recall that I mentioned a "properly structured" IUL policy. Let me explain what that means.

Remember back when we discussed the part of the IRS tax code that allows us to draw on our insurance cash value without penalty or taxes (section 7702)? Well, if you do, you will recall that this language is in the code to ensure that people don't exploit life insurance to avoid paying taxes. It is a little more involved than that, but that is essentially why the code is so specific: the government walks a balancing act of providing the insurance industry with the ability to offer the feature of tax-free access to life insurance cash value without giving up too much tax revenue from individuals who decide to utilize cash-value permanent insurance. In fact, there is a very specific term for cash-value life insurance policies that cross the line and are funded with too much money, making all of the cash-value gains within the policy taxable. That kind of policy would be called a modified endowment contract, or MEC. YOU WANT TO AVOID HAVING YOUR POLICY BE CLASSIFIED AS A MEC. That is why you need to work with a life insurance expert.

The details are involved, but you simply need to understand that every death benefit has a limited amount of cash that can be dumped into the policy on a tax-favored basis within a certain number of years. If, after your policy is issued, you want to put in more money than the MEC limit stipulates in your situation, then you will likely need to take out another policy. All insurance companies provide their licensed agents with the software needed for them to determine the SMALLEST death benefit that will accommodate the amount of cash you want to put in over a 5-, 7-, 10-, or 20-year or longer time frame.

This is the reason that the amount of Phil's death benefit is so obscure and seemingly random. It is, in fact, the absolute lowest amount of death benefit TO THE PENNY that he is able to contractually purchase **without** having that contract labeled as a MEC based on the dollar amount he planned to contribute.

This is probably one of the most, if not the most, important functional points I've made so far and one you need to remember if you decide to speak to someone about adding IUL to your long-term-savings plan. You have to insist that the policy's death benefit is the lowest amount possible, and you have to have the agent execute the contract so that it is not at risk of being labeled a MEC. Again, this is easy for the agent to do using the software provided by the insurance carrier.

Life insurance agents are paid commissions based on the total amount of death benefit. The higher the death benefit, the **higher** their commission. That is just the black and white of how they are paid. The insurance carriers want their agents selling policies with large death benefits, and agents are rewarded for doing so. Because this is the landscape of life insurance compensation for agents, you are going to have to be crystal clear with your agent as to what you are looking to achieve with the policy. In fact, you might want to give him or her a copy of this book to help spell it out.

OK, now back to our 69-year-old man, Phil.

Phil has been contributing premiums of between $20,000 and $30,000 since he opened his policy in 2006. He's been redirecting some of the long-term savings he had in one of his brokerage accounts into his policy on an annual basis. Remember that he doesn't move this money all at once because of what we just discussed, the MEC limits set by the IRS.

What I want to do here is take a look at the performance of his IUL cash balance from 2013 to 2014 based on what is called an annual crediting method (meaning his interest is credited at the end of the contract year).

At the beginning of the period, the cash balance of Phil's IUL was $234,015.15. The cash value of Phil's policy grows at a 13% cap and is shielded from loss with a 0% floor. The growth in cash value in Phil's policy is tied not to a single index but to both the S&P 500 and the NASDAQ. This is an even split, so 50% of his cash value is indexed against the NASDAQ and 50% is indexed against the S&P 500. In addition to the annual credited interest based on the two indexes' performance, a policyholder has the ability to allocate part of his or her cash value to an interest-based crediting option. The rate of return on the interest option is declared at the start of each policy anniversary year. Last, if premiums are put into a policy midway through the year, the premiums are designated to an interim account that also earns a declared interest rate until the start of the next policy year, at which time the premium is reallocated to the market-related indexes or interest-based index, however the policyholder specifies. Given these mechanics of Phil's IUL policy, let's see how it performed from December 18, 2013, to December 17, 2014.

ANNUAL STATEMENT TO POLICYHOLDER

Policy number:	
Policy date:	12/18/2006
Reporting period:	12/18/2013 - 12/17/2014
Insured:	PHIL
Gender:	Male
Issue age:	61
Class:	Select Plus Non-Tobacco
Annual planned premium:	$30,000.00
Mode:	Annual
Plan name:	

DETAIL FOR POLICY YEAR BEGINNING 12/18/2013 AND ENDING 12/17/2014

We are pleased to provide this life insurance annual statement. Your policy values as of your policy anniversary date are shown below. These values are based on your past policy year performance. We appreciate your business. If you need further assistance or have any questions, please do not hesitate to contact your representative directly, or client services at 800.950.1962, option 3.

Current Value at end of last reporting period:	(1) $234,015.51
Net premium paid:	$28,500.00 (2)
Interest credited:	(3) $23,726.67
Cost of insurance:	($1,912.96)
Cost of riders:	$0.00 (4)
Expense charge:	($90.00)
Gross partial surrenders:	$0.00
Surrender charges:	$0.00
Current Value at end of this reporting period:	$284,239.22

FIGURE 7.3. *Phil's annual statement generated on December 17, 2014. You can see opening balance, premium paid, interest credited, and all fees.*

The image above is Phil's annual statement after the interest on his cash value was applied after December 17, 2014. Keep in mind that Phil at this point was swiftly approaching 70 years of age. Let's walk through the key elements in order to get a better understanding of how Phil did with his IUL policy.

1. *Current Value:* The cash value of the policy at the beginning of this reporting period was $234,015.51.

2. *Net Premium Paid:* This is the amount that Phil contributed to the policy over the course of the reporting year: $28,500.

3. *Interest Credited:* Phil's cash value earned $23,726.67 during the previous year. We'll take a closer look at how that was calculated in just a moment, and, better yet, we'll compare this

performance to how Phil might have done if his money were in a more traditional market-aligned vehicle.

4. *Cost of Insurance (COI) and Policy Administrative Fees:* Phil paid a total of $2,002.96 for his death benefit coverage and for the administration of his policy.

Now, on that last number, the $2,002.96, we are going to get to that in some pretty good detail here, mostly because I want to dispel the myth that the cost of insurance (COI) is prohibitive to even considering this sort of approach for part of your long-term safe money. The high COI is the fear and uncertainty that traditional financial planners will want to put into your mind when you are considering IUL. But what you need to remind yourself when you ask them for their input is that you are basically wanting to pull money out of the account you have with them, and this in effect will decline the amount of your assets that they have under management, meaning they'll make less money. So, naturally, they will try to point out every potential flaw they can that is related to IUL. In a minute, I'll show why we have to look at the COI against all fees, expenses, and taxes involved in keeping this money in a traditional market-oriented investment that these advisors want you to cling to.

Before we dive into the COI, let's first take a look at the detailed performance of the policy and where the $23,726.67 came from (see Figure 7.4).

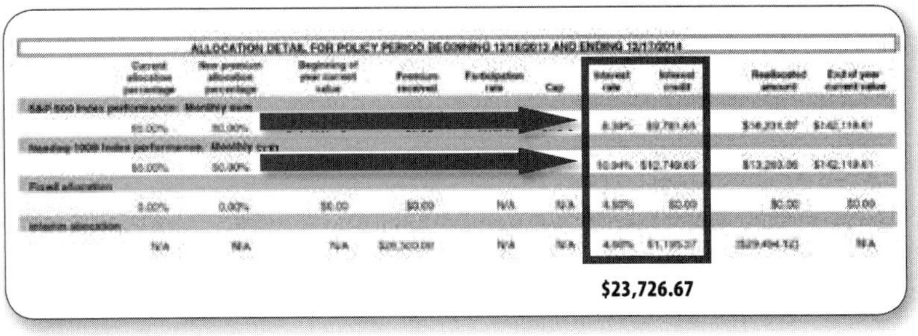

FIGURE 7.4. *So much for life insurance being too conservative. Phil's IUL policy earned 8.39% and 10.94% for the 12 previous months.*

This part of Phil's statement helps us discern how the policy works. We see that the beginning cash value of $234,015.51 has growth gains from both the NASDAQ and the S&P 500. In fact, a 50/50 split of $117,007.75 is applied to both of these indexes. The result? The $117,007.75 that was applied to the S&P 500 earned the full 8.39% that the S&P delivered over this time period, delivering a total of $9,781.65. The $117,007.75 that was applied against the NASDAQ earned the full 10.94% it delivered, for a total of $12,749.65 for Phil. And, last, the premiums that Phil paid over the year earned the interim allocation rate of 4.6%, delivering $1,195.37. The cumulative addition to Phil's IUL policy cash value is $23,726.67. So much for life insurance being too conservative like so many think. *That may have been the case for whole life insurance or universal life insurance, but being too conservative clearly does not apply to indexed universal life insurance.*

On face value, I would again argue that these proven rates of return, combined with the downside protection, are compelling enough for you to make IUL a large part of your retirement planning portfolio. Wait, however, until you better understand the return you can expect to receive from IUL in a given year when compared to the alternative. So let's walk through what Phil's $234,015.51 would have done outside the IUL in a traditional brokerage account invested in mutual funds. What we'll do here is line up all the expenses and fees on both sides of the comparison just to see an apples-to-apples comparison. What this walkthrough will do is not only better establish the benefit and value of having part of your safe money in an IUL but also help me expose the myth of a cripplingly high COI (cost of insurance).

In Figure 7.5 you'll see a typical brokerage account invested in a mutual fund that performs as good as the NASDAQ and S&P 500 return that the IUL policy delivered—a fair comparison when we consider that more than 70% of all mutual funds underperform these indexes. Where the IUL is concerned, there is the COI of $1,914 and the $90 administrative fee. In the brokerage account, we assume a fund fee of just one-tenth of a percent (i.e., 0.1%) and an advisor fee of 1%. To keep the comparison apples to apples I included the annual cost of a 10-year, $437,728 term life insurance policy for a healthy 69-year-old man. And, yes, I can hear the objections to this from where I'm typing: "But why include term? I won't be holding term at that age!" Relax on that one for a minute because I'll run these same numbers without the term insurance too. But it is absolutely fair to include it, because while we are not using the IUL necessarily for the death benefit, the death benefit is a valuable part of the asset, so it would be foolish not to include it in the comparison—especially when you better understand the impact that the death benefit has on retirement income in the long run, which we'll explain in the next chapter. Finally, we have to factor in Uncle Sam. He has to get his, after all, so I have factored in a 20% tax rate, and I think that is fair. I use 20% because we absolutely cannot, in a traditional brokerage account, avoid paying taxes. You're going to pay something, and 20% is a very reasonable number to estimate for the average individual. Some will pay less than this and some more. But even at today's current rates, the math works in the favor of the IUL no matter what rate we plug in. So as I've said earlier, drop the effort to try to expose flaws. There really are none, no matter what rate you choose. You can do the math yourself. I've chosen 20% because it simply is a good, fair number. OK, now on to the results. IUL kicks the brokerage account's butt!

MUTAL FUNDS IN BROCKERAGE ACCOUNT		INDEXED UNIVERSAL LIFE POLICY	
Beginning Balance	$234,015	Beginning Balance	$234,015
New Investment	$28,500	New Investment	$28,500
Gains	$23,727	Insurance Cost	−$1,914
Fund Fees 0.1%	−$262	Administrative Fee	−$90
Advisor Fees 1%	−$2,625	Gains	$23,727
Term Insurance	−$3,548		
Taxes (20%)	−$4,745		
TOTAL	$275,062	TOTAL	$284,238

$9,176 more in IUL

FIGURE 7.5. *The cost of insurance is a bargain compared to taxes and other out-of-pocket expenses seldom factored in with traditional investments.*

Phil is more than $9,000 to the good because he chooses to direct some of his long-term savings, a portion of his safe money, to the IUL. Is the insurance cost measurable? Of course it is, but, again, he is paying for the value here, the value of the death benefit. The big expenses on the other side of the ledger, in the brokerage account, really don't deliver any value at all. Perhaps the advisor fee of 1% delivers value if your advisor goes above and beyond and is able to alert you way ahead of market losses so that you retain what you save, but I know plenty of advisors, and most of them move money after some losses have occurred. The fact of the matter is that you get something for the COI, and even after paying it, Phil, in our example, does better than the brokerage account.

OK, let me get to one of the most common objections to my example, the cost of term life insurance. In fact, I will go one better and remove not only the cost of term insurance but also all related expenses that are generally incurred with a brokerage account. Below is the same side-by-side comparison, but I'll keep the COI and administrative fees for the IUL policy and remove **all** of the related fees for the brokerage account.

MUTAL FUNDS IN BROCKERAGE ACCOUNT		INDEXED UNIVERSAL LIFE POLICY	
Beginning Balance	$234,015	Beginning Balance	$234,015
New Investment	$28,500	New Investment	$28,500
Gains	$23,727	Insurance Cost	−$1,914
Fund Fees 0.1%	0	Administrative Fee	−$90
Advisor Fees 1%	0	Gains	$23,727
Term Insurance	0		
Taxes (20%)	−$4,745		
TOTAL	$281,497	TOTAL	$284,238

$2,741 more in IUL

FIGURE 7.6. *If you're the person who doesn't want term insurance, doesn't work with an advisor, or insists that every mutual fund you own is free from any fees, then simply compare taxes to the cost of insurance with IUL. The winner is still IUL.*

You are reading it correctly! Phil is more than $2,700 to the good because of his IUL. Why? Because the cash value that he has accumulated in the policy is not subjected to any tax at all. This is why I covered section 7702 earlier and why I took the time to explain to you how precise the tax code is around life insurance cash value and why the concept of a modified endowment contract exists. The cash value is the policyholder's to do with however he or she pleases, and the resulting growth of that cash value will never be subject to any sort of tax so long as it is accessed properly.

I used Phil as an example because of those impressions I asked you to tap into at the beginning of the chapter. Remember? I asked what you would think if I said "permanent life insurance and a 69-year-old man." The bet was that you probably thought "too expensive" or "useless" or maybe even "doesn't need it." Well, what we just walked through is a very real example of how IUL helped a 69-year-old man. And I will tell you this: Phil slept pretty easy during the 2008 crash because this money never went negative, and he was able to get much of the gain over the entire recovery period. Bottom line: Phil wasn't buying at first, either. But he saw the power of IUL, and today he is thrilled that it is part of his portfolio.

We haven't even gotten into how IUL affects retirement income, so let's take a look at that now. And that death benefit I keep saying I'll explain later, well, you're going to love what that does for you in your retirement years.

chapter 7a

Even More Compelling at Age 72

The first edition of this book was released in 2016. What you are about to see in the pages of this chapter is the sole reason for the release of the second edition. In fact, the contents of this chapter alone are enough to justify the purchase of indexed universal life for just about any human being healthy enough to obtain it. Not only that but also the contents of this chapter are enough to blow to smithereens the strongest of rebuttals to owning IUL from any advisor, attorney, accountant, or any other person you know who thinks they know their stuff when it comes to finances. I would implore you to let any so-called financial expert read this chapter all by itself and have him or her put in writing why you shouldn't purchase indexed universal life.

A few years have passed since Phil's annual IUL statement was issued and used in the previous chapter. It is late summer of 2018 as I type this. As you can see from Phil's annual IUL statement issued on December 17 of 2017 in Figure 7.a.1, Phil is now 72 years old. Again, the policy was issued in 2006, when Phil was 61 years old. Do the math, and you can determine that Phil was 72 when this annual IUL statement was issued to him.

ANNUAL STATEMENT TO POLICYHOLDER

Policy number:	
Policy date:	12/18/2006
Reporting period:	12/18/2016 - 12/17/2017
Insured:	PHIL
Gender:	Male
Issue age:	61
Class:	Select Plus Non-Tobacco
Annual planned premium:	$30,000.00
Mode:	Annual
Plan name:	

DETAIL FOR POLICY YEAR BEGINNING 12/18/2016 AND ENDING 12/17/2017

We are pleased to provide this life insurance annual statement. Your policy values as of your policy anniversary date are shown below. These values are based on your past policy year performance. We appreciate your business. If you need further assistance or have any questions, please do not hesitate to contact your representative directly; or client services at

Current Value at end of last reporting period:	(1) $313,506.79
Net premium paid:	$0.00 (2)
Interest credited:	(3) $66,717.56
Accumulation Value bonus:	$1,047.43 (4)
Minimum monthly premium bonus:	$0.00
Cost of insurance:	(5) ($1,407.34)
Cost of riders:	$0.00
Expense charge:	(5) ($90.00)
Gross partial surrenders:	$0.00
Surrender charges:	$0.00
Current Value at end of this reporting period:	$379,774.44 (6)

FIGURE 7.a.1. *Page 1 of Phil's 2017 annual IUL statement.*

The numbers are different in this annual statement compared to the one issued in 2014. Let me explain each one.

1. Phil's policy started the year with $313,506.

2. Phil paid zero premiums the previous year. Premiums for IUL do not have to be paid every year, unlike other kinds of life insurance. As long as there is enough cash value to cover the annual insurance fees, premiums do not have to be paid.

3. Phil's policy earned $66,717 based on the performance of the S&P 500 and NASDAQ 100 the previous 12 months. That is a 21% rate of return! This smashes the notion that life insurance is too conservative of an investment. Whole life insurance is too conservative, and so is universal life. Indexed universal life can deliver great returns for the policy holder WITH ZERO RISK of loss from stock market declines, as this annual statement proves even more than it did in the previous chapter. I will point out how Phil earned 21% in a few paragraphs.

4. This particular insurance company paid Phil a $1,047 bonus because the policy is more than 10 years old. This is an insurance carrier's way of rewarding its policyholder for keeping the policy in force. Not every insurance company offers this bonus, and even this insurance company is not obligated to pay it every year, and for that reason I will ignore it in the math I will do in the following paragraphs. But paying an annual bonus each year after the policy is 10 years old is the insurance carrier's way of getting a leg up on its competition.

5. Phil's policy incurred a total of $1,497 of insurance fees and expense charges.

6. At the end of the year, Phil's cash value is now $379,774.

Let's tie all of the above together. Something tells me you already may have done the math. If Phil earned $66,717 in any taxable investment (such as mutual funds that many of you reading this own in a brokerage account with Vanguard or Fidelity), he would have had to pay taxes on those gains. For the sake of argument, let's assume Phil would have been taxed at 20%. To remind you, my client Phil is a high-income earner and would have had to pay a tax bill a lot higher than 20%. A 20% tax on the $66,717 gains earned in a taxable investment means that Phil would be on the hook for a $13,343 tax bill on the gains. Would he be upset? Of course not. Neither would you. I'd gladly pay $13,343 in taxes if I earned $66,717. But Phil doesn't have to pay ANY taxes on the $66,717 of interest credited in his IUL policy thanks to section 7702 of the Internal Revenue Code. He does, however, have to pay $1,497 of insurance-related fees and expenses. What a shame for Phil.

So, drumroll please. What would you rather pay? $13,343 in taxes or $1,497 in insurance fees? Another no-brainer. Of course, you'd take the $1,497 in insurance fees, and so would your accountant, attorney, advisor, or that super genius know-it-all friend of yours. They just have to get over that fact that we are talking about life insurance. To be more specific, a properly designed indexed universal life policy in which the death benefit is the smallest allowed by the IRS that still allows it to be classified as life insurance.

On to the rest of Phil's IUL annual statement. So how did his policy earn such a high rate of return? See Figure 7.a.2.

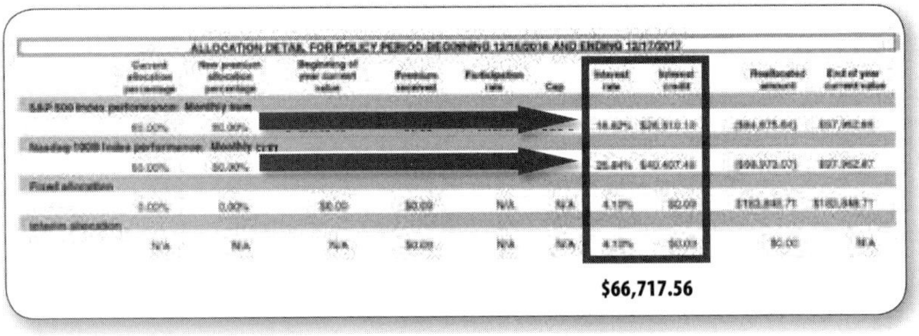

FIGURE 7.a.2. *Page 2 of Phil's 2017 annual IUL statement.*

Phil allocated 50% of his money to the S&P 500 and 50% to the NASDAQ 100 index. He could have allocated money to the fixed account, which pays 4.10% annually, but he didn't. By the way, these allocations can be changed by the policyholder once a year within 30 days of the policy anniversary date.

Phil earned 16.82% with the money allocated to the S&P 500 and a 25.84% rate of return for the money allocated toward the NASDAQ 100. Add those figures together and your blended rate of return is about 21%. Fantastic! So much for the notion that life insurance is a bad investment.

The Death Benefit Keeps Rising

Take a look at Figure 7.a.3. It represents page 3 of Phil's annual statement. There are a couple key things I want to point out.

The first is the death benefit in the upper right-hand corner. Notice once again how it is an odd dollar amount. This death benefit of $546,875.19 represents the smallest death benefit down to the penny that Phil could have and still have the policy classify as life insurance. We covered the "smallest death benefit" concept in chapter 7, so I won't repeat it again. I do, however, want you to compare the $546,875 death benefit in Figure 7.a.3 with Phil's death benefit from his 2014 annual statement that is in Figure 7.2 on page 90.

In 2014, Phil's death benefit was $437,728.40. Three years later in 2017 you can see it has increased by $109,146 and is up to $546,875. Why is that? The death benefit is always higher than the cash value. As the cash value increases, the death benefit increases too. Is that a big deal? Absolutely! In chapter 9 you will learn why the death benefit is a key component in your overall retirement plan, and the proof of how it increased for Phil over the past three years will solidify what you learn in that upcoming chapter.

CURRENT POLICY COVERAGES			
INSURED	BENEFITS		SPECIFIED AMOUNT
PHIL	BASIC DEATH BENEFIT		* $546,875.19
	TERMINAL ILLNESS RIDER		

DEATH BENEFIT OPTION: A

"A" The Total Death Benefit is equal to the Basic Death Benefit above

"B" The Total Death Benefit is equal to the Basic Death Benefit plus Accumulation Value

*The Basic Death Benefit amount above will be reduced by any outstanding loan balance prior to distribution.

THE FOLLOWING TABLE SHOWS THE CALCULATION OF THE SUM OF CAPPED MONTHLY RATES DURING THE PAST YEAR.

Month	*S&P 500 Index	Capped monthly rate	*Nasdaq - 100® Index	Capped monthly rate
12/18/2016	2,258.07	N/A	4,914.86	N/A
01/17/2017	2,267.89	0.434%	5,044.65	2.640%
02/17/2017	2,351.16	3.500% ✓	5,324.72	3.500%
03/17/2017	2,378.25	1.152%	5,408.76	1.578%
04/17/2017	2,349.01	(1.229)%	5,399.19	(0.170)%
05/17/2017	2,357.03	0.341%	5,580.54	3.358%
06/17/2017	2,433.15	3.229%	5,681.47	1.808%
07/17/2017	2,459.14	1.068%	5,839.73	2.785%
08/17/2017	2,430.01	(1.184)%	5,790.31	(0.743)%
09/17/2017	2,500.23	2.889%	5,967.99	3.306%
10/17/2017	2,559.36	2.364%	6,122.61	2.248%
11/17/2017	2,578.85	0.761%	6,314.51	3.134%
12/17/2017	2,675.81	3.500% ✓	6,466.32	2.404%

Sum of capped monthly rates 16.820%
Interest rate: 16.820%

Sum of capped monthly rates 25.840%
Interest rate: 25.840%

*Market values are effective as of the market open on the given date.

FIGURE 7.a.3. *Page 3 of Phil's 2017 annual IUL statement.*

OK, stop. Let me emphasize a point one last time before I continue with the rest of this chapter. Everything you've just read from the beginning of this chapter until this paragraph is as good as it gets pertaining to why every person who is healthy enough to obtain his or her own indexed universal life policy should go ahead and get one. EVERYONE! The rest of this book will provide even more education as to how IUL works and how it should be used in someone's overall financial plan.

It is common for people like you to ask the opinions of others pertaining to indexed universal life. Brace yourself, because if you do, you will encounter a lot of funny looks due to the fact that very few people understand how cash-value life insurance works, specifically IUL. When you do, hand them this book and force them to read this chapter all by itself. If you still get a funny look after they read and review Phil's annual statement, then you should give them a funny look back as you realize that perhaps these people are not as financially savvy as you thought.

Other Index Crediting Methods

Perhaps you are asking how Phil earned 21% when the upside caps on IUL are in the 11%–15% range, based on what you have read thus far in this book. Most insurance companies offer multiple crediting methods in their IUL policies for clients to choose from. Up until now, I have referenced what is referred to as the "annual point-to-point" crediting method. "Annual point-to-point" refers to an index such as the S&P 500 with a floor of anywhere between 0% and 2% and an upside annual cap on that same index of 11%–15%. Many insurance companies have annual point-to-point methods that are tied to the S&P 500, the NASDAQ 100, the Dow Jones, the Russell 2000, and others. The most popular index is, without question, the S&P 500.

I have focused on the annual point-to-point index crediting method thus far for two reasons. First, I didn't want to overwhelm you and spend too much time on the different crediting methods that are available to you with IUL. I wanted to focus on how IUL works, with a floor and ceiling, the tax treatments, and the liquidity. Second, my favorite index crediting method is the annual point-to-point. It is more predictable and has consistently delivered higher returns than any other interest crediting method. Fact is most carriers have several index options for the policy holder to choose from.

One such interest crediting methodology is what is referred to as a "participation rate." Here is how it works. Suppose an insurance company offers a 50% participation rate tied to the S&P 500. If over the next 12 months the S&P 500 gains 12%, you would earn 6%, or 50% of the 12% annual gains. If the index earned 30% over the next year, then you would be credited 15%. If the index was negative, you would not lose anything and earn whatever the floor was, which in most cases is 0%.

The last crediting method that I will cover (there are few other less popular ones) is "monthly point-to-point." This is the index that Phil chose for his policy. At the beginning of the policy year, the insurance company states the monthly caps for the next 12 months. For Phil, during the policy year from December 18, 2016, through December 17, 2017, his monthly cap was 3.5%. That means that each month, the most Phil can earn is 3.5%. Take another glance at Figure 7.a.3. Phil hit his monthly cap twice, as you see where the check marks are indicated. This index has the ability to deliver some really great returns. In theory, if the stock market earned 3.5% every single month over the course of a year, then the index would credit 42% (3.5% × 12 months = 42%). In the event there are more negative months than positive months, then you are once again protected and would be saved by a 0% floor.

Why wouldn't everyone pick the monthly point-to-point crediting method if the upside is so great? The reason is because it can also be very inconsistent. With the monthly point-to-point crediting method, you are given a cap on the monthly gains you can receive, BUT THERE IS NO MONTHLY FLOOR on how much you can lose each month. See Figure 7.a.4.

Notice how in Figure 7.a.4. you would be capped at 3.5% monthly gains during the good months, but there is no floor as to how much the index can drop each month, as was the case in June, July, and October. In the event the index has a negative total at the end of the year, you would still be protected by a 0% floor.

	Hypothetical S&P 500 Monthly Gains/Losses	Monthly Point-to-Point with 3.5% Cap
January	2	2
February	2.5	2.5
March	4	3.5
April	5	3.5
May	-2	-2
June	-6	-6
July	-5	-5
August	5	3.5
September	4	3.5
October	-5	-5
November	2	2
December	5	3.5
TOTAL	**11.5**	**6**

FIGURE 7.a.4. *A monthly point-to-point crediting method caps you on the gains each month but does not limit your losses each month.*

So what crediting method is the best? The market behaves differently each year, and as a result each crediting method will do better or worse than the others at different times. Personally speaking, as long as you can get an upside cap on the annual point-to-point crediting method of at least 11% on the S&P 500, then that is my first choice. It has proven to be the most consistent crediting method of them all.

chapter 8

More for You and Less for the IRS

I believe the three examples we walked through to illustrate the power of the mechanics of IUL are powerful enough for anyone to seriously consider leveraging it as an important tool in his or her retirement savings strategy. We have taken a close look at how the policy's cap and floor allow the holder to benefit from positive movement in the market and completely avoid any risk of market volatility with the lock and reset feature. We also looked at the benefit that IUL had for one of my clients who purchased his policy at age 61 and how he is way ahead of the game some twelve years later for doing so.

In that latter example, I touched on the benefit of tax-free access to the cash value in the policy. This works because of the IRS regulations I discussed a few chapters back, specifically, IRS Code 7702. This section of IRS code qualifies the cash value in a life insurance asset as a wholly owned asset of the policyholder—an asset that the holder is free to do with as he or she wishes, including borrowing against the total value of the asset. Think of it as home equity. After all, you are free to do what you want with the equity in your house, and if you draw money against home equity, in the form of a home equity loan, you are not required to pay tax on that cash. Now, of course, with a home equity loan you are indebted to pay interest to the financial institution that granted you access to your home's equity. But the IUL policy is an asset that provides the policy owner with access to the cash value that is growing in the policy. And the beautiful thing about accessing your policy's cash value is that there is no need to justify why you want the money. Imagine doing that with a bank. Think about what happens anytime you want to borrow money from a bank, or anywhere else for that matter. You need to justify why you need the money and how the money will be repaid. Not so with the cash value within all life insurance policies, not just IUL. If you have $150,000 of cash surrender value and you want access to $20,000 of it to buy a car or to use as a down payment on an investment property, you just pick up the phone and call the insurance company to get the money. You'll need to put your request in writing on a loan or withdrawal form, but it's an easy process. The money is in your hands generally within a week.

Now, to be clear, this is in no way to suggest that you should treat your IUL as an ATM of sorts. That would not be prudent. IUL should be mentally treated with the same sort of discipline that you treat your 401(k). My strong advice is for you to touch the money within the policy BEFORE RETIREMENT only if you plan on repaying the cash value back into the policy. We want our cash value to reap as much of the benefit of positive stock market movement as possible, because when we reach retirement, we will want the option of exercising the right to access this cash tax free, with no intent to pay it back to the policy, and use it to supplement our retirement income. It is here where the real power of the tax-free benefit makes a serious impact. Let's take a closer look.

To better appreciate the benefit, we'll consider the policy of a 50-year-old man and examine how the same total annual savings amount over the course of 15 years stacks up when he begins to draw on that savings. Here are the assumptions that we are going to make:

Annual Investment or IUL Premium ($1,000 a month):	**$ 12,000**
Assumed Yearly Interest in Brokerage Account:	**8%**
Assumed Yearly Brokerage fee:	**0.35%**
Assumed Performance of the IUL:	**7.5%**
Tax Bracket:	**28%**
Death Benefit of IUL Policy:	**$207,792**

Before I go any further, let me address the two assumed performance numbers. We are going to give the brokerage account a pretty good "benefit of the doubt" sort of number of 8%. In other words, we're assuming this 50-year-old earns 8% on his brokerage account for not just the next 15 years, but every year for the rest of his life.

Let's also forget, for the purpose of our example here, that people move their money to more conservative positions the closer they get to retirement age. So not only are you unlikely to get a year-over-year 8% return but also, if you are like every other average investor, you'd most certainly not have your money positioned to get this kind of return when you get to your late 50s or early 60s. This is absolutely intentional because I want to remove all possible buts, what-ifs, and wait-a-minutes from the conversation. So I have heavily favored the market performance here—so much, in fact, that it would be my hope that you come away thinking something like, "Wow, that example was pretty compelling. But it is even more compelling because the market scenario he used is never gonna happen." What about the 0.35% fee that will be accompanying the 8% returns that I will be using? Is that fair? Well, how about you pick up the phone and call your local Merrill Lynch or Ameriprise Financial office or any traditional brokerage firm in your area. Ask to speak to the BEST ADVISOR in the office. I assure you that advisor is charging anywhere from 1% to 2.5% annually to handle the portfolio of his or her clients. Heck, when you call, ask to speak with the advisor just hired out of college and who has ZERO experience. I promise you this rookie will charge you at least 0.50% to manage your money. So is my 0.35% fee that is being factored in fair? Absolutely! Am I stacking the deck in my favor? Well, you be the judge. I would argue that I am stacking the deck in the favor of the brokerage account. It just so happens that the IUL's performance makes sense even in the face of an absolute best-case scenario for the brokerage account.

Bottom line is this: if we knew that we'd get around an 8% return every single year, most of us would be thrilled, even with a 0.35% advisor fee.

As far as the IUL performance number of 7.5% is concerned, I would point you back to chapter 5 ("Lifting the Hood"). I shared with you some statistical probabilities of IUL performance over a 20-year period. Those numbers indicated that IUL would credit its cash value a year-over-year return between 7% and 7.5% nearly 95% of the time. That is a pretty good track record since 1968. I want to make sure that you feel comfortable with the 7.5% assumption that I'm giving to the IUL policy in the comparison that I am about to use. Here is a more thorough look at how IUL has stacked up against the S&P 500 from 1930 to 2009. I realize this may be a little redundant to what we covered in chapter 5, but it is critical that you truly understand why IUL will deliver a consistent credit of 7%–8% over most 5-, 10-, 20-, or 30+-year time horizons.

What you are going to be looking at is a chart of 12 different three-decade periods of comparison between the S&P 500's historical performance and an IUL policy with a 13% cap and a 0% floor. I assumed a specific amount of money invested every year for 30 years in both scenarios. You can validate my numbers in this exercise using data that can easily be found on the Internet.

See Figure 8.1 for the results.

YEAR	S&P 500	IUL 13% CAP/ 0% FLOOR
1930–1959	7.71	7.13
1935–1964	8.54	7.47
1940–1969	7.73	7.23
1945–1974	4.19	6.53
1950–1979	4.63	6.71
1955–1984	4.69	6.81
1960–1989	7.13	7.67
1965–1994	7.2	7.1
1970–1999	11.83	8.57
1975–2004	9.73	7.89
1980–2009	7.05	7.56
1985–2014	7.72	7.98

FIGURE 8.1. *IUL consistently credits between 6.5% and 8.5% during most 30-year lookback segments of the market.*

I love this chart. I use it in my seminars, and I play a little game with the audience. The 30-year-period results are covered up, and I ask the audience to pick a time where they think the market will far outperform the IUL. I do about three different periods and then reveal them all. Needless to say, the audience is surprised at how well the IUL does, and they are even more thrilled to learn that the growth happened with absolutely no market downside exposure. The point of the exercise, as I just mentioned, is to help the audience get comfortable with the 7.5% number. I hope it has done the same for you.

So, just as I overestimated the performance of the stock market to remove any excuses for why the comparison might be unfair, I took a conservative approach with the IUL based on history. Time and again, the IUL delivers right around the 7.5% mark. This is why I use 7.5% when I illustrate IUL performance.

OK, now that you understand the assumptions, let's get back to our 50-year-old man and take a look at how his $12,000 a year does in his brokerage account. See Figure 8.2.

BROKERAGE ACCOUNT

YEAR	(1) ANNUAL DEPOSIT TO THE ACCOUNT	(2) AFTER-TAX CASH FLOW FROM THE ACCOUNT	(3) PRE-TAX INVESTMENT INCOME	(4) AFTER-TAX INVESTMENT INCOME	(5) YEAR-END ACCOUNT VALUE
1	12,000	0	960	691	12,646
2	12,000	0	1,972	1,420	25,972
3	12,000	0	3,038	2,187	40,016
4	12,000	0	4,161	2,996	54,815
5	12,000	0	5,345	3,849	70,411
6	12,000	0	6,593	4,747	86,847
7	12,000	0	7,908	5,694	104,167
8	12,000	0	9,293	6,691	122,419
9	12,000	0	10,754	7,743	141,653
10	12,000	0	12,292	8,850	161,923
11	12,000	0	13,914	10,018	183,283
12	12,000	0	15,623	11,248	205,794
13	12,000	0	17,423	12,545	229,515
14	12,000	0	19,321	13,911	254,514
15	12,000	0	21,321	15,351	280,857

FIGURE 8.2. *Column 5 represents the after-tax (28%) and after-advisor-fee (35%) net, assuming a 50-year-old man invests $1,000 monthly ($12,000 annually) into a taxable account, assuming he receives an 8% return every single year.*

So how does the brokerage account do with all of our favorable assumptions? At the end of his 15-year investing period, he has $280,857.

Now let's compare the same $12,000 annually in an IUL policy crediting 7.5%.

IUL POLICY

	(6)	(7)	(8)	(9)	(10)
YEAR	POLICY PREMIUM	AFTER-TAX POLICY LOAN PROCEEDS	YEAR-END ACCUM VALUE*	YEAR-END SURRENDER VALUE*	DEATH BENEFIT
1	12,000	0	10,241	3,488	218,033
2	12,000	0	21,019	14,401	228,811
3	12,000	0	32,531	26,048	240,323
4	12,000	0	44,783	38,570	252,575
5	12,000	0	57,825	51,883	265,617
6	12,000	0	71,741	66,068	279,533
7	12,000	0	86,565	81,162	294,357
8	12,000	0	102,365	92,367	310,157
9	12,000	0	119,236	114,644	327,028
10	12,000	0	137,304	133,117	345,096
11	12,000	0	159,377	155,730	367,169
12	12,000	0	183,096	180,125	390,888
13	12,000	0	208,704	206,408	416,496
14	12,000	0	236,351	234,865	444,143
15	12,000	0	266,229	265,554	474,021

FIGURE 8.3. *If $1,000 monthly ($12,000 annually) is deposited into an IUL contract, assuming a 7.5% annual credit, you would have totals similar to those shown above.*

The year-end accumulation (column 8) represents the dollar amount that is credited with gains (if any) from the index. The year-end surrender value represents the dollar amount the consumer would receive should he or she cancel the policy. As you can clearly see, the year-end accumulating value in the first three to five years stacks up horribly against the brokerage account. In fact, the policy is actually underwater until about year five. The reason for this, of course, is that we have to pay for the value of the death benefit on the policy. This is why I spent time on the COI (cost of insurance) earlier. The COI, in the long run, doesn't even come close to what we pay in brokerage fees, advisor fees, and taxes. While that is true, however, we have to understand that in IUL, we are investing for the long haul. It is not a place to put money that you need in the next five years or so. If you were saving for a swimming pool, for instance, you wouldn't want to park that savings in an IUL policy.

The real strength of the policy can be seen after the 15-year savings period when this 50-year-old man begins to draw on his account balances. It is important to realize that you, the policyholder, can access money from your policy at any time, with no justification to anyone at the insurance company home office as to why you want it. Imagine that. Try doing that at the bank. After all, it's your money. You can take any

IUL POLICY

YEAR	POLICY PREMIUM	AFTER-TAX POLICY LOAN PROCEEDS	YEAR-END ACCUM VALUE*	YEAR-END SURRENDER VALUE*	DEATH BENEFIT
16	0	30,755	286,543	253,943	441,420
17	0	30,755	308,694	241,538	406,863
18	0	30,755	332,803	229,017	370,234
19	0	30,755	359,012	216,398	331,406
20	0	30,755	387,497	203,726	290,249
21	0	30,755	418,515	191,117	253,894
22	0	30,755	452,171	178,529	237,311
23	0	30,755	488,595	165,935	219,681
24	0	30,755	528,047	153,427	200,951
25	0	30,755	570,814	141,116	181,073
26	0	30,755	617,215	129,135	159,996
27	0	30,755	667,336	117,371	150,738
28	0	30,755	721,473	105,909	141,983
29	0	30,755	779,931	94,833	133,830
30	0	30,755	843,036	84,233	126,384
31	0	30,755	911,123	74,191	119,747
32	0	30,755	984,562	64,813	114,041
33	0	30,755	1,063,739	56,206	109,393
34	0	30,755	1,149,068	48,482	105,936
35	0	30,755	1,240,971	41,750	103,798
TOTAL		615,100			

FIGURE 8.4. *Assuming a 7.5% annual credit, the IUL policy can generate $30,755 starting in year 16 (age 66) and do so every year until year 35 (age 85).*

amount out up to the cash surrender value. You can take out different amounts each year. You can pay the money back that you take out if you want. It is up to you.

For this example (see Figure 8.4), I utilized the insurance company's illustration software to generate the amount of money the policy can spit out each year from ages 66 to 85 (years 16–27), assuming the policy credits 7.5% each year. Let's take a look at Figue 8.4

What we find is that our 50-year-old man can take out $30,755 TAX FREE from age 66 to age 85—20 years, which totals $615,100. And what of the brokerage account?

BROKERAGE ACCOUNT

YEAR	POLICY PREMIUM	AFTER-TAX POLICY LOAN PROCEEDS	YEAR-END ACCUM VALUE*	YEAR-END SURRENDER VALUE*	DEATH BENEFIT
16	0	30,755	20,008	14,406	263,563
17	0	30,755	18,625	13,410	245,338
18	0	30,755	17,167	12,360	226,131
19	0	30,755	15,630	11,254	205,892
20	0	30,755	14,011	10,088	184,562
21	0	30,755	12,305	8,859	162,085
22	0	30,755	10,506	7,565	138,399
23	0	30,755	8,611	6,200	87,132
24	0	30,755	6,615	4,762	87,132
25	0	30,755	4,510	3,247	59,411
26	0	30,755	2,292	1,651	30,198
27	0	30,198	0	0	0
28	0	0	0	0	0
TOTAL		368,503			

FIGURE 8.5. *When taxes and advisor fees are factored in, the brokerage account runs out of money at age 78 (year 28) if the same $30,755 is withdrawn.*

If this man draws the same $30,755 a year as part of his overall retirement income, this brokerage account is drained to zero when he is 78 years old (year 28 on the chart above). The total that he would have used as income on that account would have been about $360,500. That is eight fewer years of cash flow and $246,597 less in actual cash.

Let's take a look at it side by side (see Figure 8.6).

	Annual Draw Amount	Number of Draw Years	Additional IUL Income Years	Total Retirement Income	% More Income from IUL
Brokerage	$30,755	12		$368,503	
IUL	$30,755	20	8	$615,100	68%

FIGURE 8.6. *IUL generates 68% more money than the brokerage account.*

For the same exact $12,000 over the same number of years, the IUL delivers an additional eight years of supplemental income for a total of 68% *more* cash for the 50-year-old man to spend and enjoy. This is the power of the favorable tax treatment from the IRS on your cash-value life insurance. It literally extends your income beyond what you could possibly hope to gain from the traditional long-term-savings approach.

Let me dive into a couple of things that always comes up in my seminars when I walk through this same example. First, taxes—specifically, the 28% bracket I'm using for the example. "28%?!?" some shout at me as if I'm trying to pull one over on them. "The tax rate on the $30K won't be 28%!" We need to be clear on this: the $30,755 is an income *supplement*, not a sole source of income. Could the taxes be lower (or even higher)? Absolutely, but they are going to be there. There is no avoiding them. So I've picked 28%, and it is a fair number, *especially* when you consider how favorably I've treated the brokerage account. So feel free to cling to the tax rate I've selected as the one hang-up that you just can't get past to justify why you wouldn't consider IUL a strategic part of your long-term plan. I personally think it's foolish to do so, but, hey, I'm not here to strong-arm anyone into seeing things my way.

No, I am just trying to get the information out because my experience tells me that most people have no idea that such a powerful financial vehicle like IUL exits.

The second point is the $30,755. Some want to know why that amount. It is an important question and underscores the way you should arrive at how your IUL policy should be structured. When considering IUL for a client, we'll typically use a 20-year window to see how much his or her retirement income can be increased and improved by using a properly structured policy. That is what we have done in this case, and then we lined up the resulting draw against what we could potentially draw on the same money invested in a brokerage account. We can dial this number up or down, start the draw later or earlier, make the draw period longer or shorter. The takeaway ought not to be the $30K but the better results on the draw from the IUL when compared to the brokerage account.

One last point here on the tax favorability of the policy. I have explained the way the IRS code works and the importance of structuring the policy in order to be able to take advantage of this tax treatment. To simplify all of this, however, I think it is best to look at the IUL draw table in Figure 8.4 and notice that the death benefit is decreasing each year from the point that the withdrawal begins. This is the reason why there are absolutely no taxes on the policy. It is the death benefit that receives the favorable tax treatment. The policyholder in this case is, in essence, receiving an advance on his or her income-tax-free death benefit, thanks to section 7702 of the Internal Revenue Code. This is the mechanics of the IUL that can be utilized to your advantage.

So, we've looked at some real-life examples that illustrate the power of the lock and reset feature of IUL, especially during heavy periods of stock market volatility. We stepped through an example of a

69-year-old-man and how his policy has performed better than he could have done in a traditional brokerage account, dispelling the myth of high and unreasonable cost of insurance along the way. And now we have taken a look at how the IUL would potentially add more than 50% to a policyholder's retirement income. Are you convinced that you should take steps to sort out how you can effectively add IUL to your long-term-savings strategy? I'm betting that you are, but if you are not, I have one more reality of IUL to step through that will answer the challenge of avoiding living a frugal retirement because we are scared of outliving what we've saved.

In the next chapter, we'll illustrate how IUL should be integrated into your retirement income plan so that you can spend and enjoy more of your retirement savings and give a lot less to the IRS. When it comes to putting together A Better Financial Plan, the next chapter is as good as it gets.

chapter 9

Retirement Income Planning Checkmate

Want A Better Financial Plan? Then make a properly designed indexed universal life policy a part of your portfolio and you'll instantly have just that. A properly structured IUL contract is safe from loss, and the cash surrender value is liquid. IUL will deliver you good returns without the need to constantly reposition your cash value every time there is a crisis around the globe. Last, IUL will generate tax-free income to you, thanks to section 7702 of the Internal Revenue Code. The past few chapters proved all of this to you. What you've read up until now should have more than convinced you to make IUL 25%–50% of your portfolio. To use a golf analogy, IUL is the golf club—the best golf club on the market. This chapter is going to teach you the retirement planning golf swing. In the event you had any question whatsoever as to whether IUL should be a major piece of your retirement plan, this chapter will more than convince you.

For the next several pages, I need you to forget about IUL or anything we have covered in this book so far. We will tie it all together toward the end of the chapter, but, for now, just clear your mind pertaining to financial planning.

SPEND AND ENJOY

Regardless of your age or risk tolerance, why are you putting, or why did you put, money away for retirement? Seems like an easy enough question, doesn't it? Most people have a similar answer to this question, while at the same time their answer isn't as specific as it should be.

Most people say "so I have money to live off of when I stop working" or something similar. If I ask for more specifics, I hear things like "so I don't run out of money." Seldom are the answers to this question much more detailed than this. How about you? Before you keep reading, specifically, answer, Why are you saving money for retirement? Can you articulate it?

Well, here is why I say people save for retirement: "to have enough money when you stop working so that you can maintain the same lifestyle as you did prior to retirement without the fear of outliving your money."

Agree?

It's probably not far off from what you were thinking, but it's just a little more specific. Retirement planning is not about getting to retirement with the biggest bucket of money. Obviously, the more money you accumulate, the better. But, again, more importantly and specifically, it's about having as much money as you can accumulate, positioned in such a way that you can spend and enjoy enough of it to maintain your same lifestyle without the fear of outliving it. That is a mouthful, I know.

But I think it captures what most people are trying to achieve during retirement. Very few people, however, are in a position to do this, and most advisors have no idea how to teach their clients the solution to this problem.

We just clarified what we want during retirement. So why, then, is running out of money the number one fear of seniors? These are the same seniors who have followed the prevailing wisdom of socking away all they could in qualified plans and riding out the stock market volatility until it becomes time to draw on that savings.

We'll dive into that question soon enough, but I'd like to ask you to place a mental bookmark on the question by placing a face (faces, actually) on the issue.

FIGURE 9.1. *Which couple would you like to be? Although most people want to leave money to their children, spending and enjoying their money are higher priorities.*

Take a look at the photos in Figure 9.1 and of these two senior couples and answer another very important question: which of these two couples would you rather be? Couple A or couple B?

Look, I'll admit it: I stacked the deck here by showing the pictures. Invoking a laugh is always a good idea when you are presenting, but, more importantly, the exaggeration of the look of the two couples underscores a point. Bottom line is this: do you want to spend and enjoy your money or live frugally? It really is that simple. Everyone wants to spend and enjoy. Couple A is the couple who is fearful of running out of money, and having this fear limits their retirement lifestyle. They likely travel less frequently than they would like, if at all, and they dine out less, go to the movies less, etc. From a financial perspective, they see their day-to-day as a constant ledger of the dollars and cents they will need for the next year, the next month, the next day. They become shackled to their account balances as the anxiety over their retirement income grows.

Everyone wants to be couple B. Everyone wants to spend and enjoy his or her money during retirement. Yes, everyone would like to leave his or her children money, but living frugally in order to do so is not a priority for most seniors.

The sad truth is that you are most likely on a path to becoming couple A and NOT couple B. Let me prove why.

Let's assume you are 65 years old and just retired. You have a $1 million nest egg accumulated. Now, it doesn't matter whether you have $100,000, $1 million, or $10 million at age 65. The problem and the solution are the same. What does every senior do with his or her portfolio upon retirement? He or she gets more conservative with the money. Everyone knows that. So let's also assume you earn a 5% rate of return. Don't worry about how you earn 5% for now; just assume 5% because for the past 30 years you likely earned 8%–10% investing in the stock market (or so you thought). Next question: how long does your million have to last until? Well, there is only one correct answer. It needs to last until you and your spouse pass away. And since we don't know when that will be, I suggest to all of my clients that they plan on having their money last until age 90 or 95. Anything short of that is foolish. Believe me: I realize two things. It is very likely that you and your spouse will die long before 95. I also realize that you will have more fun with the money between ages 65 and 75 than you will between 75 and 85. That being said, you can't put a financial plan together to be broke at age 80. I hope you agree.

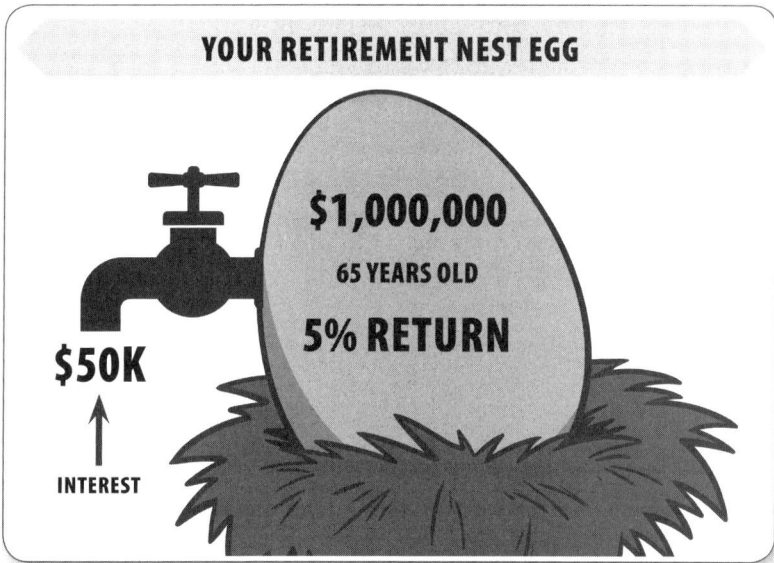

YOUR RETIREMENT NEST EGG

$1,000,000

65 YEARS OLD

5% RETURN

$50K

↑ INTEREST

FIGURE 9.2. *On the surface, living off the interest makes sense. You never outlive your nest egg. The $1,000,000 nest egg generates $50,000 of annual income. Not bad!*

Let's continue with traditional retirement planning. It's likely that this couple will live off the interest that their $1 million generates. Why? First of all, everywhere you look, the so-called experts are telling you that this is what seniors should do. Remember that the number one fear of seniors is outliving their money. If you just live off the interest, then your principal is never touched, which obviously means you won't outlive your money. And since all the experts are saying to do this, then living off the interest must be the best thing to do. A 5% rate of return on $1 million is $50,000 every year. So, on the surface, that's not so bad. This couple simply needs to learn how to get by with $ 50,000 annually. Not the end of the world. But here is the important question: WHO IS SPENDING THE $1 MILLION? You? No! Your kids are! You're COUPLE A!

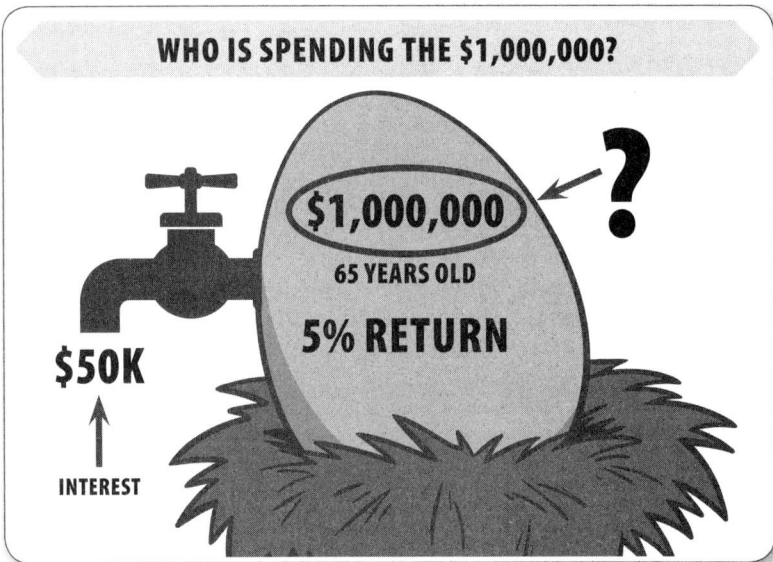

FIGURE 9.3. *The problem is this: who spends the $1,000,000? You? No! Your kids do. You're couple A!*

Do you now understand the dilemma every retired couple faces, regardless of the size of their next egg? Everyone wants to spend down and enjoy his or her money, but nobody knows how much to spend for fear of outliving it. So what happens? People live more frugally with their money than they need to. They "live off the interest." Traditional advisors promote this strategy. Why? Because all of these Wall Street–related companies and their advisors are collecting recurring revenue on your retirement nest egg as it sits under their management. No wonder they don't tell you to go spend it. It would be a pay cut for them.

I've asked every one of my seminar attendees over the years for a solution to this retirement-planning quandary. I ask for a show of hands of who knows how to solve this problem. Nobody has ever raised a hand. Can you figure it out? You will see in a minute that the solution is incredibly simple, as I promised it would be in the beginning of the book.

At my seminars, I'll pick out a married couple in the audience and look directly at the man and ask him this question:

"If you knew that your spouse was guaranteed to be taken care of financially when you pass away due to a large life insurance death benefit, what can you selfishly do with the rest of the money while you're alive?"

The guy that I pose the question to will smirk, shift in his seat, pause for a second, and say "SPEND IT!" I'm telling you that 99.9% of the time, the answer I get back is "spend it." *IN FACT, THERE IS ONLY ONE ANSWER TO THIS QUESTION, AND THAT IS "SPEND IT"!*

Did the lightbulb just go off in your head? There isn't another single financial move that you can make that will cause you to spend and enjoy more of your money with less fear of outliving it during retirement than guaranteeing the financial security of your spouse utilizing the death benefit from life insurance. This is retirement planning checkmate!

Go ahead: try to poke a hole in that strategy. You can't. Nobody can. And because you can't, that's why you need to implement this for yourself.

Now, I need to make an assumption with you. I need to assume that you love your spouse—I mean really love your spouse and care about her or his financial well-being. That may seem like a silly question, but you'd be surprised. I see a lot of people in my office. I come across a few people a year (men) who have the attitude of "My wife will be fine when I go. She can figure it out." If you have that same attitude, well, then, you're the kind of person who may not put any value in this chapter.

So, a quick summary and then we will get to some actual numbers that will blow you away.

Guys (sorry, ladies, using the guy in my example since he likely will die first), only two things can happen to you during retirement. You are going to die young, at, let's say, age 73, or you are going to die at a nice old age of, let's say, 88.

With a properly structured IUL policy in force, if you die at 73, your wife gets the balance of your mutual fund investments and all of your other assets, AND a week later the death benefit payout that comes from the IUL insurance company. I joke with the wives in my office when I explain this. I tell them to "act sad at the funeral." Or, if both husband and wife get into their 80s and have depleted the rest of their assets, they then start to take money out of the IUL policy tax free to live off of. I already proved to you that while you are spending your other assets, the cash within the IUL policy will be growing and compounding tax free, getting good returns with no risk of market loss. And when you start taking money from the policy, it will spit out 35%–50% more money net of taxes than any other investment you have.

Why Not Just Buy Term Insurance?

As stated earlier, I feel that 99% of adults are underinsured. Term would help just about every family properly protect themselves from an unexpected death. If you did nothing else after you read this book but go out and buy the proper amount of term insurance to protect your family, then I've helped you significantly.

I hope, however, that you can put two and two together as to why term insurance doesn't work for retirement planning and why cash-value life insurance is needed to make this strategy work. You need a large death benefit for your spouse should you die young, but you also need the cash value provided inside IUL to maximize what you can spend and enjoy should you reach an old age. Term life insurance doesn't work because it only provides a death benefit that is incredibly expensive to own during retirement. Term is so expensive during retirement that very few people can afford to keep it. Hence, that is why so few term policies actually pay out.

The Numbers

Let me show you how easy it is to turn a couple from couple A to couple B and the benefits that come with the transition.

Couple A, Live off the Interest

COUPLE A	LIVE OFF THE INTEREST
Let's assume the following:	
Age of Male:	**50**
Current Nonqualified Mutual Fund Balance:	**$250,000**
Monthly Savings Moving Forward:	**$ 1,000**
Retirement Age:	**65**

FUTURE VALUE	
Present Value:	$ 250,000
Monthly Payment:	$ 1,000
Number of Months:	180
Annual Interest:	8.00%
Future Value:	$1,175,075

FIGURE 9.4. *If couple A starts with $250,000 at age 50 and saves $1,000 a month for the next 180 months (15 years), they will have accumulated $1,175,075 at age 65 assuming an 8% rate of return.*

As I have been doing in all of our examples, I want to give the mutual fund account the absolute best benefit of the doubt. So we are going to award this couple an 8% annual rate of return for every year they place $1,000 monthly savings into a nonqualified mutual fund account for the next 15 years. I know, I know: they'll never get it, but that is OK. We want to look at the absolute best-case scenario because you'll see when we are wrapped up here that even that is most likely not an argument for staying the course with traditional long-term retirement savings.

So if you whip out your financial calculator, you will see that 15 years later, when this man is 65 years old, the resulting balance in the mutual fund account would be **$1,175,075.**

Let me remind you of the financial dilemmas this couple faces. First, they can't afford to lose money at age 65, so they get more conservative with their nest egg. Just about every senior does. Assume moving forward they earn 5% on their money. Again, forget where or how they are getting a 5% return. The other issue they face is that they are not sure how much they can spend each year. Their money needs to last until they both pass away, and since they don't know when that will be, they need to make sure their money lasts until at least 90 or 95 years of age. Yes, I agree that all of us want to and will likely be able to enjoy the money more between the ages of 65 and 75. But to put a financial plan together to be broke at age 80 is just plain stupid. I don't know how else to say it.

Here's another important question. Do you agree with the following opinion of mine?

> "I'm not worried about leaving my kids a ton of money, but I also don't want to be a financial headache to them, either."

My experience tells me that most couples agree with that thinking. So, bottom line: couple A in this scenario needs to have their money last 25–30 years. One more question. Would it be crazy to think that over the next 25–30 years couple A might experience a stock market crash? How about an illness that impacts one of the two of them? Is it feasible that one of couple A's children would experience a hardship such as illness, divorce, or long-term unemployment? I hope you agree that it is VERY likely that one or more of these events could hit couple A, which will without question negatively impact their finances. We all know retirees, maybe in our immediate family, who need to financially help out another family member due to an unexpected hardship. My point is this: couple A can't aggressively spend their money for fear of outliving it. So, whether they realize it or not, couple A lives off the interest and tries to leave their principal intact.

OK, having stressed all of that, let's get to the numbers.

Here is what retirement income will look like for couple A based on that mutual fund balance of **$1,175,075** and a "***never run out of income, live off the interest***" strategy. Again, assume a 5% rate of return without this couple ever losing any money.

COUPLE A
MUTUAL FUND RETIREMENT INCOME

ASSETS: $1,175,075   5% EARNED INTEREST   —   TAX BRACKET: 28.00%

AGE	GROSS WITHDRAWAL	ANNUAL TAX	NET INCOME
65	58,754	(16,451)	42,303
66	58,754	(16,451)	42,303
67	58,754	(16,451)	42,303
68	58,754	(16,451)	42,303
69	58,754	(16,451)	42,303
70	58,754	(16,451)	42,303
71	58,754	(16,451)	42,303
72	58,754	(16,451)	42,303
73	58,754	(16,451)	42,303
74	58,754	(16,451)	42,303
75	58,754	(16,451)	42,303
76	58,754	(16,451)	42,303
77	58,754	(16,451)	42,303
78	58,754	(16,451)	42,303
79	58,754	(16,451)	42,303
80	58,754	(16,451)	42,303
81	58,754	(16,451)	42,303
82	58,754	(16,451)	42,303
83	58,754	(16,451)	42,303
84	58,754	(16,451)	42,303
85	58,754	(16,451)	42,303
86	58,754	(16,451)	42,303
87	58,754	(16,451)	42,303
88	58,754	(16,451)	42,303
89	58,754	(16,451)	42,303
90	58,754	(16,451)	42,303
91	58,754	(16,451)	42,303
92	58,754	(16,451)	42,303
93	58,754	(16,451)	42,303
94	58,754	(16,451)	42,303
95	58,754	(16,451)	42,303
TOTALS	**1,821,366**	**(509,983)**	**1,311,384**

FIGURE 9.5. *Couple A "lives off the interest." Assuming a 5% rate of return and a 28% tax bracket, couple A's $1,175,075 nets $42,303 every year from age 65 to age 95. The kids inherit the $1,175,075.*

To make this projection more realistic, we need to factor in the impact of taxes. Assume a 28% tax bracket. Again, let's not split hairs as to which tax bracket is best to use. I hope you agree I've been more than fair with every scenario in this book. Given these assumptions, Figure 9.5 shows the cash flow looks like this from 65 to 95:

To ensure that they never run out of money, couple A will essentially be drawing 5% of their balance each year. This keeps the entire principal intact and yields an after-tax income of $42,303. Over the course of his 30 years of retirement, assuming he lives until 95, our 50-year-old man spends about $1,311,384 and pays about $509,983 in taxes.

COUPLE B, Spend and Enjoy

Here is where it gets really good. Using the same starting point as couple A, let's take a look at the difference a properly structured IUL policy will make to this 50-year-old man's retirement income.

Couple B, just like couple A, will be saving $1,000 a month until age 65. The difference, however, is that that money will be redirecting into an IUL contract for the next 15 years. No change in cash flow, just a redirection of the monthly savings. Simple enough.

Once again, take out your financial calculator to confirm my math. The mutual fund balance of $250,000 at age 50, with no further contributions, grows to $826,730 at age 65, assuming it earns 8% every single year.

FUTURE VALUE	
Present Value:	$250,000
Monthly Payment:	0
Number of Months:	180
Annual Interest:	8.00%
Future Value:	$826,730

FIGURE 9.6. *Couple B, starting with the same $250,000 at age 50, diverts the $1,000 monthly savings toward an IUL policy. Fifteen years later, $250,000 growing at 8% each year is worth $826,730.37 at age 65.*

Age	Year	Planned Premium Outlay	Withdrawals/ Loans	Account Value	Surrender Value	Net Death Benefit
				Non-Guaranteed Assumptions **Current Interest of 7.50%** **End of Year**		
51	1	12,000	0	7,653	0	511,709
52	2	12,000	0	15,810	4,610	511,709
53	3	12,000	0	24,511	13,900	511,709
54	4	12,000	0	33,808	23,787	511,709
55	5	12,000	0	43,747	34,315	511,709
56	6	12,000	0	54,382	45,540	511,709
57	7	12,000	0	65,780	57,528	511,709
58	8	12,000	0	78,000	70,337	511,709
59	9	12,000	0	91,114	84,040	511,709
60	10	12,000	0	105,203	98,718	511,709
		120,000	**0**			
61	11	12,000	0	122,594	116,699	511,709
62	12	12,000	0	141,361	136,645	511,709
63	13	12,000	0	161,630	158,093	511,709
64	14	12,000	0	183,530	181,172	511,709
65	15	12,000	0	207,086	205,907	511,709
66	16	0*	0	220,904	220,904	511,709
67	17	0*	0	235,738	235,738	511,709
68	18	0*	0	251,710	251,710	511,709
69	19	0*	0	268,895	268,895	511,709
70	20	0*	0	287,418	287,418	511,709
		180,000	**0**			
71	21	0*	0	307,297	307,297	511,709
72	22	0*	0	328,659	328,659	511,709
73	23	0*	0	351,688	351,688	511,709
74	24	0*	0	376,601	376,601	511,709
75	25	0*	0	403,672	403,672	511,709
76	26	0*	0	433,162	433,162	511,709
77	27	0*	0	465,431	465,431	511,709
78	28	0*	0	500,819	500,819	525,860
79	29	0*	0	539,050	539,050	566,003
80	30	0*	0	580,130	580,130	609,136
		180,000	**0**			
81	31	0*	75,979	624,256	544,699	575,912
82	32	0*	75,979	671,657	508,794	542,377
83	33	0*	75,979	722,569	472,478	508,607
84	34	0*	75,979	777,243	435,815	474,677
85	35	0*	75,979	835,940	398,873	440,670
86	36	0*	75,979	898,936	361,726	406,673
87	37	0*	75,979	966,525	324,455	372,781
88	38	0*	75,979	1,039,021	287,152	339,103
89	39	0*	75,979	1,116,762	249,922	305,760
90	40	0*	75,979	1,200,114	212,889	272,894
		180,000	**759,790**			
91	41	0*	75,979	1,289,415	176,133	240,604
92	42	0*	75,979	1,385,999	140,724	196,164
93	43	0*	75,979	1,490,634	107,149	151,868
94	44	0*	75,979	1,604,187	75,982	108,066
95	45	0*	75,979	1,727,636	47,895	65,172
96	46	0*	0	1,862,057	103,201	103,201
97	47	0*	0	2,006,945	165,246	165,246
98	48	0*	0	2,163,114	234,671	234,671
99	49	0*	0	2,331,442	312,170	312,170
100	50	0*	0	2,512,877	398,497	398,497
		180,000	**1,139,685**			

FIGURE 9.7. *Couple B diverts $1,000 a month into an IUL policy for 15 years. The policy can generate $75,979 of income, tax free, each year from ages 81 to 95.*

This mutual fund balance is $348,345 *less* than what couple A has.

But, *in addition to* the mutual fund account, couple B has an IUL policy in force with a death benefit at age 65 of $511,709 and a liquid cash value of $205,907. This assumes that the IUL policy credits 7.5% (and in the previous chapters I have more than proved that 7.5% is a fair rate to use). This cash value grows tax free, will have the ability to earn double-digit returns, and has no market exposure. Who in their right mind doesn't want that for a large piece of their retirement portfolio? The illustration from which the IUL numbers come from is shown in Figure 9.7.

Remember that the IUL death benefit is what you are paying for. In this case, if our 50-year-old man unfortunately passes away the day after he writes his first check to the insurance carrier, the entire $511,709 death benefit is delivered to his beneficiary, most likely his spouse, tax free. That is compelling, but it's not the only purpose of why we use IUL to augment our retirement income. So let's see how couple B's retirement looks until age 95 and then compare it to couple A's.

More Aggressive Draw

Now couple B is 65 years of age (assume both husband and wife are age 65). This couple hopes that they both live a healthy retirement and are able to make it 30 more years. Statistically speaking, the husband will die first. He has the peace of mind knowing that when he passes away, his wife will receive his $511,709 death benefit in addition to the other assets they have. Guess what? His wife has peace of mind for the same reasons as her husband.

Because couple B has the death benefit in place, they can more aggressively spend their money. It's that simple. It's a psychological way of thinking. It's not based on any calculator. This psychological fact is what trips up so many people and traditional advisors.

"My spouse will financially be OK when I die because of the death benefit. Because of that fact, we can more aggressively spend the rest of our money while we are both alive."

You agree with that last statement; I know you do. Did you need to grab a calculator and crunch numbers before you bought into that philosophy? Nope. You didn't. That's why you need to get to retirement with an IUL policy in force. Too many people crunch numbers trying to determine whether they can get a better return investing their money in other things. Don't be one of those people. Don't overcomplicate it. Put some of your money into IUL, and then go blow the rest!

The plan for couple B is to spend their $826,730 mutual fund balance from ages 65 to 80—all of it! We'll keep all the same assumptions as for couple A. They are receiving a more conservative 5% rate of return on their traditional investments, and the cash value in IUL grows at 7.5%. Remember that there is no reason to get conservative with the IUL's cash value because the built-in floor of the policy will prevent you from experiencing another 2008.

Take a look at the annual cash flow flow in Figure 9.8. Pay particular attention to the annual taxes.

Notice how the amount of taxes you pay to the federal government decreases every year. Why is that? Remember that couple B is drawing not just the interest on the account but both interest and principal. In fact, couple B is drawing down $76,282 each year from ages 65 to 81. *That is $17,000 more a year than couple A.* This decreases the principal, *which has the effect of decreasing the tax burden, as they are taxed on the gains of their principal.* And since couple B is spending down their principal balance, the principal earns less interest. Since it earns less interest, couple B has less tax. Since couple B has less tax, they keep more money each year. So as the costs of milk and bread and gas rise each year,

COUPLE B
IUL RETIREMENT INCOME

ASSETS: $826,730   5% EARNED INTEREST   —   TAX BRACKET: 28.00%

AGE	GROSS WITHDRAWAL	ANNUAL TAX	NET INCOME
65	76,282	(11,574)	64,708
66	76,282	(11,085)	65,197
67	76,282	(10,571)	65,711
68	76,282	(10,032)	66,250
69	76,282	(9,466)	66,817
70	76,282	(8,871)	67,411
71	76,282	(8,246)	68,036
72	76,282	(7,591)	68,692
73	76,282	(6,902)	69,380
74	76,282	(6,180)	70,103
75	76,282	(5,421)	70,862
76	76,282	(4,624)	71,659
77	76,282	(3,787)	72,495
78	76,282	(2,908)	73,374
79	76,282	(1,986)	74,297
80	76,282	(1,017)	75,265
81	75,979	(0)	75,979
82	75,979		75,979
83	75,979		75,979
84	75,979		75,979
85	75,979		75,979
86	75,979		75,979
87	75,979		75,979
88	75,979		75,979
89	75,979		75,979
90	75,979		75,979
91	75,979		75,979
92	75,979		75,979
93	75,979		75,979
94	75,979		75,979
95	75,979		75,979
TOTALS	**2,360,202**	**(110,260)**	**2,249,942**

FIGURE 9.8. *Assuming the same 5% rate of return and 28% tax bracket, couple B spends down principal and interest from ages 66 to 80. The tax liability decreases each year due to the fact that they are taxed on the gains of their principle, which allows them to net out more money. Once this "mutual fund" account is depleted, couple B takes money from their IUL policy tax free.*

so does the amount couple B keeps after taxes, sort of like an inflation hedge. So as couple B spends down and enjoys their retirement savings, they are rewarded with a smaller tax bill.

Under this plan, when couple B gets to age 81, they will likely be out of money within their traditional investments. If so, they pick up the phone and call their IUL insurance company and start borrowing income-tax-free money from their life insurance each year, which in this case is $75,979 (Figure 9.7). They can withdraw this amount every year through age 95 (again, assuming a 7.5% credit to the policy). As they take money from their policy, the net death benefit starts to drop because in the insurance company's eyes, the money they take out is in essence an advance on the death benefit it owes them. It's OK that the death benefit drops a little bit now that they are in their 80s. After all, every year that goes by is one less year that the surviving spouse would need the money as well.

So how does couple B compare to couple A (see Figure 9.9) The drumroll, please:

It's not even close. Couple B, spending and enjoying more of their hard-earned savings, spends about 72% MORE MONEY and pays about one-fifth the taxes as couple A.

Too good to be true? How about you take the numbers you see here and cut them in half. What if you spent only 36% more money during retirement with less risk and no change in your cash flow? Would you sign up for that? I sure hope so.

Let's focus on the kids in this example for a second. What if the husband passes away at age 85? As you can see in Figure 9.7, a tax-free death benefit of $440,670 passes to his wife, assuming she is still alive. Something tells me the kids will still likely get a piece of that death benefit.

WHICH COUPLE DO YOU WANT TO BE?

COUPLE A

COUPLE B

Gross Income: $1,821,366
Taxes Paid: ($504,983)
Net Income: $1,311,384

Gross Income: $2,360,202
Taxes Paid: ($110,260)
Net Income: $2,249,942

72% MORE INCOME – 1/5 THE TAX

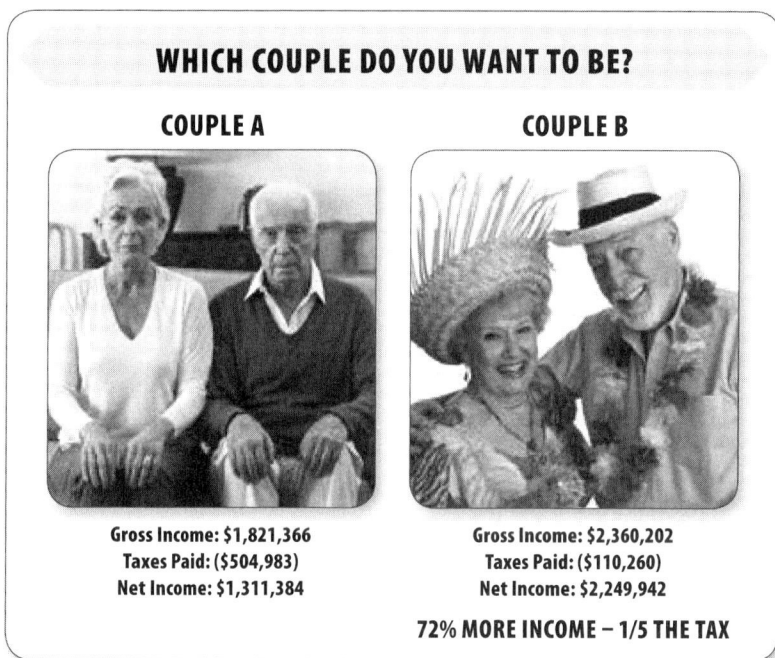

FIGURE 9.9. *Couple B spends 72% more money than couple A and spends about one-fifth the taxes.*

Example 2, Couple B for a 65-Year-Old Couple

The previous example was based on a 50-year-old man, still working, still able to save. The numbers were compelling—really compelling. Make no mistake: the earlier you create your IUL policy, the better. That being said, assuming you are healthy enough, it is seldom too late to purchase an IUL policy and become couple B. Remember that it's not about a math equation. It's a mind-set. Can't a 60- or 70-year-old man come to the same conclusion to the question we posed earlier? Here it is again. *My spouse will financially be OK when I die because of the death benefit. Because of that fact, we can more aggressively spend the rest of our money while we are both alive.* Of course he can. Let me prove it using numbers on a 65-year-old male who just got done reading this book.

COUPLE B	A 65-YEAR-OLD COUPLE
Let's assume the following:	
Age of Male:	**65**
Current Nonqualified Mutual Fund Balance:	**$1,000,000**
Monthly Savings Moving Forward:	**$ 0**
Retirement Age:	**Today**

This couple has $1 million and earns 5% on their money moving forward, is in a 28% tax bracket, and simply lives off the interest for fear of outliving their money. We covered all the reasons they are scared to spend down their money earlier, so let's just focus on the numbers. See Figure 9.10 for couple A.

Couple A, as you can see in Figure 9.10, spends $36,000 after taxes every year from ages 65 to 95. During that period of time, they spend $434,000 in taxes and net out $1,116,000. If they spend more than that each year, they run the risk of outliving their money.

So how would this couple A become couple B?

They simply transfer $50,000 from their mutual funds over to an IUL policy each year for five years, which totals $250,000. This amount creates a good-size death benefit and still leaves this couple plenty of money to spend over the next few years as the cash value of their policy grows without market risk. See Figure 9.11 to see what the policy would look like.

COUPLE A
MUTUAL FUND RETIREMENT INCOME

ASSETS: $1,000,000   5% EARNED INTEREST   —   TAX BRACKET: 28.00%

AGE	GROSS WITHDRAWAL	ANNUAL TAX	NET INCOME
65	50,000	(14,000)	36,000
66	50,000	(14,000)	36,000
67	50,000	(14,000)	36,000
68	50,000	(14,000)	36,000
69	50,000	(14,000)	36,000
70	50,000	(14,000)	36,000
71	50,000	(14,000)	36,000
72	50,000	(14,000)	36,000
73	50,000	(14,000)	36,000
74	50,000	(14,000)	36,000
75	50,000	(14,000)	36,000
76	50,000	(14,000)	36,000
77	50,000	(14,000)	36,000
78	50,000	(14,000)	36,000
79	50,000	(14,000)	36,000
80	50,000	(14,000)	36,000
81	50,000	(14,000)	36,000
82	50,000	(14,000)	36,000
83	50,000	(14,000)	36,000
84	50,000	(14,000)	36,000
85	50,000	(14,000)	36,000
86	50,000	(14,000)	36,000
87	50,000	(14,000)	36,000
88	50,000	(14,000)	36,000
89	50,000	(14,000)	36,000
90	50,000	(14,000)	36,000
91	50,000	(14,000)	36,000
92	50,000	(14,000)	36,000
93	50,000	(14,000)	36,000
94	50,000	(14,000)	36,000
95	50,000	(14,000)	36,000
TOTALS	**1,550,000**	**(434,000)**	**1,116,000**

FIGURE 9.10. *Couple A "lives off the interest." Assuming a 5% rate of return and a 28% tax bracket, couple A's $1,000,000 nets $36,000 every year from age 65 to age 95. The kids inherit the $1,000,000.*

		Planned Premium Outlay	Withdrawals/ Loans	Account Value	Surrender Value	Net Death Benefit
Age	Year					
				Non-Guaranteed Assumptions **Current Interest of 7.50%** **End of Year**		
66	1	50,000	0	36,966	6,563	542,516
67	2	50,000	0	76,752	47,870	542,516
68	3	50,000	0	119,732	92,370	542,516
69	4	50,000	0	166,325	140,483	542,516
70	5	50,000	0	217,004	192,682	542,516
71	6	0*	0	224,247	201,445	542,516
72	7	0*	0	231,809	210,527	542,516
73	8	0*	0	239,744	219,982	542,516
74	9	0*	0	248,107	229,866	542,516
75	10	0*	0	256,970	240,249	542,516
		250,000	**0**			
76	11	0*	0	268,962	253,760	542,516
77	12	0*	0	281,926	269,765	542,516
78	13	0*	0	296,007	286,886	542,516
79	14	0*	0	311,367	305,286	542,516
80	15	0*	0	326,945	323,904	542,516
81	16	0*	0	343,375	343,375	542,516
82	17	0*	0	360,961	360,961	542,516
83	18	0*	0	380,025	380,025	542,516
84	19	0*	0	400,840	400,840	542,516
85	20	0*	0	424,615	424,615	542,516
		250,000	**0**			
86	21	0*	64,268	451,805	384,549	475,260
87	22	0*	64,268	482,636	344,995	404,876
88	23	0*	64,268	517,960	306,663	332,561
89	24	0*	64,268	555,957	267,578	295,376
90	25	0*	64,268	596,720	227,675	257,511
91	26	0*	64,268	640,447	186,985	219,007
92	27	0*	64,268	687,893	146,089	173,604
93	28	0*	64,268	739,347	105,092	127,272
94	29	0*	64,268	795,275	64,271	80,176
95	30	0*	64,268	856,219	23,967	32,529
		250,000	**642,680**			
96	31	0*	0	922,790	51,838	51,838
97	32	0*	0	994,544	83,092	83,092
98	33	0*	0	1,071,885	118,051	118,051
99	34	0*	0	1,155,247	157,060	157,060
100	35	0*	0	1,245,101	200,498	200,498
101	36	0*	0	1,341,951	248,774	248,774
102	37	0*	0	1,446,342	302,332	302,332
103	38	0*	0	1,558,860	361,655	361,655
104	39	0*	0	1,680,140	427,264	427,264
105	40	0*	0	1,810,863	499,729	499,729
		250,000	**642,680**			

FIGURE 9.11. Couple B transfers $50,000 each year for five years from their taxable investment account to a $542,516 death benefit IUL policy, which is able to generate more than $64,000 tax free from ages 86 to 95.

Why not just put $250,000 into an IUL policy in one lump sum? See for yourself in Figure 9.12.

| | | Planned Premium Outlay | Withdrawals/ Loans | Non-Guaranteed Assumptions Current Interest of 7.50% End of Year | | |
| | | | | Account Value | Surrender Value | Net Death Benefit |
Age	Year					
66	1	250,000	0	182,046	30,033	2,894,625
67	2	0*	0	0	0	0
		250,000	**0**			

FIGURE 9.12. *If couple B dumps $250,000 into an IUL policy in the first year, the death benefit jumps to $2,894,625. The internal costs associated with such a large death benefit will cause the policy to lapse in the second year.*

If $250,000 is dumped into the policy in year one, the smallest death benefit is $2,894,625. Because the death benefit is so large, the internal insurance costs and other related fees are so high that they cause the policy to lapse in the third year. Dumping $250,000 into a policy in one year is the equivalent to doing a cannonball in the deep end of a swimming pool—we've all seen the splash and the waves created. Instead, the more efficient thing for couple B to do is put $50,000 into a policy for five consecutive years. That's the equivalent of waddling into the pool in the shallow end—no splash, no waves. Putting the money into the policy over five years allows for the death benefit to be one-fifth as large and simultaneously have far fewer internal fees.

Let's compare the two scenarios again. See Figure 9.13.

Once again, it's not even close. Between the ages of 65 and 95, couple B spends and enjoys $1,737,156 compared to couple A's $1,116,000. That's a 56% increase in spending for couple B as a result of paying about $300,000 LESS in taxes. Cut those numbers in half. If couple B spends

COUPLE B
IUL RETIREMENT INCOME

ASSETS: $750,000   5% EARNED INTEREST   —   TAX BRACKET: 28.00%

AGE	GROSS WITHDRAWAL	ANNUAL TAX	NET INCOME
65	58,497	(10,500)	47,997
66	58,497	(10,206)	48,291
67	58,497	(9,897)	48,600
68	58,497	(9,573)	48,924
69	58,497	(9,233)	49,264
70	58,497	(8,876)	49,621
71	58,497	(8,501)	49,997
72	58,497	(8,107)	50,390
73	58,497	(7,693)	50,804
74	58,497	(7,259)	51,238
75	58,497	(6,803)	51,694
76	58,497	(6,324)	52,173
77	58,497	(5,821)	52,676
78	58,497	(5,293)	53,204
79	58,497	(4,739)	53,758
80	58,497	(4,157)	54,340
81	64,268	(3,546)	54,593
82	64,268	(2,904)	55,593
83	64,268	(2,230)	56,267
84	64,268	(1,523)	56,974
85	64,268	(780)	57,717
86	64,268	(0)	64,268
87	64,268		64,268
88	64,268		64,268
89	64,268		64,268
90	64,268		64,268
91	64,268		64,268
92	64,268		64,268
93	64,268		64,268
94	64,268		64,268
95	64,268		64,268
TOTALS	**1,871,119**	**(133,963)**	**1,737,156**

FIGURE 9.13. *Assuming the same 5% rate of return and 28% tax bracket, couple B spends down principal and interest from ages 66 to 85. Once this investment account is depleted, couple B takes money from their IUL policy tax free.*

only 28% more money with less risk and no cash flow change, would that be good enough for you? I sure hope so.

So there you have it. You now know how to spend and enjoy significantly more money during retirement. The numbers are extremely compelling. I hope you agree. Before I forget, let me tell you that this strategy works with any set of numbers. You may have half the amount saved or twice the amount I used in my examples. It is all relative. You just need to work with a competent advisor who can help you build the policy that is right for you, based on your monthly savings and/or the amount of money you have in your nonqualified accounts.

chapter 10

A Better Financial Plan

I think it is time for a review. I have thrown a lot at you, I know. In chapter 1, I made some bold promises to you. I bet you thought that they all sounded too good to be true. I hear it all the time at my seminars. Now would be a good time to review each of them to see whether I delivered.

In chapter 1 I promised:
Increased liquidity

The cash surrender value of life insurance is liquid. Putting all of your money into 401(k)s and IRAs is not. The combination of reducing your contributions to qualified retirement plans and purchasing an IUL policy increases your liquidity.

Increased protection from unexpected financial hardships

If you lose your job, aren't you better off having access to more money? Think about it. Try getting a loan from the bank if you are unemployed. Banks prefer lending money to people who are working. The same goes if you become disabled. When a financial hardship hits, the cash value in your IUL policy buys you time, doesn't it? Of course it does. I'm not saying it will last forever, but it will buy you time, and that makes you better off.

Will deliver a good rate of return on your long-term savings

I proved this multiple ways using IUL statements from actual clients and back-testing numerous 10-, 15-, 20-, and 30-year periods of the S&P 500, assuming there was cap and floor, as is the case with IUL.

Pay less taxes during retirement—a lot less!

Chapter 8 proved this to you, and so did chapter 9, covering couple A and couple B. If that didn't prove how tax efficient this plan is, then I give up.

Pay less fees to traditional advisors

There are no annual advisor fees when you buy IUL—as in ZERO. You can't beat zero.

Dramatically reduce the amount of time you spend managing your retirement plan

Why do people spend time allocating and then reallocating their mutual fund portfolios? They are trying to maximize their gains and minimize their losses. People would probably do just as well if they wore a blindfold during this exercise. IUL makes it simple. When the S&P 500 loses money, you are protected, as I proved using Tom's 2008–2009 annual statements in chapter 6. When the index does well, your money shares in all of the gains up to the cap. What could be easier? No reason to spend any time managing this asset. Go spend all the extra time with your family.

Spend and enjoy 30%–50% more money during retirement

Once again, I proved this in chapters 8 and 9. If you know your spouse will be taken care of by a big tax-free death benefit when you die, what can you selfishly do with the rest of your money? SPEND IT!

Easily accomplish all of the above while *reducing* your overall investment risk and without changing your cash flow one bit

A Better Financial Plan is easy to implement because all you need to do is redirect some of your monthly savings or transfer some of your lump-sum investment dollars to IUL. Your risk of loss is for the most part eliminated, as I proved in chapter 6 using the 2008–2009 annual statements for my client Tom.

I hope I've made my case for adding indexed universal life to your portfolio. This fantastic financial instrument should make up 25%–50% of your portfolio. If someone tells you otherwise, particularly another advisor, ask him or her to put the reasoning in writing. Most likely this person won't. But on the slim chance he or she did, you will be able to poke holes in the reasoning with one, if not several, of the chapters in this book.

You should put money into IUL because it makes sense for the financial benefits I outlined in all of the previous chapters. Having said all that, the liquidity of all cash-value life insurance allows you to take advantage of other investment opportunities that present themselves to you along the way. And I assure you, if you keep an eye out for them, there will be plenty from which to choose. Chapter 11 will help me make that point.

chapter 11

Be the Bank

Indexed universal life makes up 50% of my current net worth. It's the Swiss Army knife of financial vehicles in that it is capable of providing multiple benefits to me at the same time. The death benefit protects my wife and children from financial hardship in the event of my untimely death. The cash-value growth provides tax efficiency, protection from loss, and a very high likelihood of a steady rate of growth that will provide me a tax-free income during retirement.

In addition to everything I've listed in the preceding paragraph, cash-value life insurance provides me with liquidity. I've mentioned this before, but liquidity is such an important element to financial success that I feel the need to dedicate an entire chapter to make my point.

There is no better way to illustrate the power of cash value's liquidity than to tell you a few of my own real-life successes using the cash value of my own policy. You'll get a better feel for who I am and the power of this tremendous financial vehicle.

I bought my first life insurance policy in 1992, a whole life policy. Keep in mind that indexed universal life wasn't invented by the insurance industry until the early 2000s. When I eventually got into the life insurance industry full time in 2004, I rolled all of my whole life cash values into an IUL policy. Although I was happy with my whole life policies, I had a hunch that IUL's upside potential and downside protection would be an even better way to go than whole life. It turns out I was right.

I bought my initial whole life policy from a buddy of mine named Rich. Can't say I understood why I bought it—probably just to get him to stop calling me. I remember having to meet Rich every year to be reminded as to the benefits of owning the policy. I was constantly questioning my decision to buy it because I was putting the same amount of money into the stock market and the returns of the market were killing the returns of my life insurance policy. Remember how well the market did in the '90s? It seemed like every mutual fund was earning 25% a year or more.

As I earned more money at work, I saved more each month. I was always a good saver. I bought another whole life insurance policy from Rich simply to satisfy the thinking that I couldn't put all my eggs in the stock market basket. Besides, my wife and I were having kids, and I needed additional life insurance coverage. My premiums were $500 a month. When Rich walked me through the benefits of owning cash-value life insurance, it always seemed to make so much sense. He taught me about tax-free growth and access to my money should I ever need it. My skepticism about the policy came when I left his office. Every time I told people I owned cash-value life insurance, they looked at me like I was stupid. I felt I was, particularly when I would look at how well my 401(k) was performing during the late '90s.

Fast-forward to the spring of 2000. What started to happen? The market started to tank. And unlike in 2008 when the market got crushed for one year, the correction of 2000 lasted for three years. Do you remember? Bet you do. I remember being scared to turn on the radio when I left work for fear of hearing about how far the market had fallen that day. There was, however, one silver lining in my portfolio: my whole life insurance policy. The cash value inside the policy kept going up and up and up. Not by 25%, like the market had done each year in the '90s, but it was going up nonetheless. All of a sudden I had a new respect for life insurance.

Cash-Value Life Insurance Allowed Me to Seize the Moment

Even though the stock market was going through some tough times from 2000 to 2002, the real estate market around the country was doing well, and the Philadelphia suburbs were no exception. It seemed everyone else was making money in real estate back then, so why couldn't I have my own success? My kids were young, and I had no shortage of energy, so I thought I'd give it a go. I had one problem. Where was I going to get the money to invest in real estate? I was doing what everyone else was doing in that I was contributing money to my nonliquid 401(k), so that was no help. Besides, its value was way down due to the market correction happening, and, after all, that was for retirement. Aha! What about the cash value of my life insurance policy? I can use that! And I did. I borrowed money from my life insurance policy to buy a small piece of land not far from my home. I hired a builder and built a house. Actually, a builder built the home; I wrote the checks. Bottom line: I cleared about

$40,000 on the sale of that house. And that was AFTER I put everything back into my policy that I had borrowed. Not bad. Start to finish, it took me fewer than six months to make that money. So what do you think I did? That's right: I did it again and again.

The cash value of my life insurance policy acted as my line of credit for every real estate purchase I made. Over the next couple years, the stock market continued to decline, but my real estate investing success continued. From 2001 to 2006 I bought 11 parcels of land and constructed and sold 11 homes. My average profit per home was about $45,000. In addition to the homes I built, I acquired 15 rental properties, hired a builder to rehab them, and rented them out. At one point these rentals were clearing about $5,000 a month. Again, my cash-value life insurance served as my line of credit for much of the real estate acquisitions. I would take the money from the policy to use as down payments on the homes, as well as for paying for the materials and labor needed to fix them up. Once fixed up, the houses were appraised for 30%–50% more than I paid for them. I would then do cash-out refinances and pay back my life insurance policy, and the tenants would pay the mortgage. What was great about taking money from my life insurance policy was how easy it was. There was no need to justify to some insurance company executive or loan officer why I needed the money and no need to provide my credit score or anything else. When I called to get the money from my policy, I had to sign a form and check one of two boxes on how I wanted to receive my check, overnight mail or regular mail. That was about as hard as it got.

Cash-Value Life Insurance Helped Support a Career Change

Let's back up a minute. From 2000 to 2003 I was working in the ERP software consulting business. I worked for Deloitte Consulting and Anderson and a small boutique company by the name of Intelligroup. During those three years, I was not shy discussing my new favorite financial savings vehicle, cash-value life insurance (indexed universal life wasn't created yet; we'll get to that soon). Keep in mind that the market was on a three-year losing streak. The funny thing was that the same people who laughed at me during the '90s when they found out I owned cash-value life insurance were eager to learn about it now that the stock market was experiencing a major correction. They also wanted to know how I leveraged my policy to make money in real estate. I was amazed that nobody I spoke with knew how cash-value life insurance worked—I mean NOBODY!

I must have referred 30 coworkers to my life insurance agent, Rich, during that three-year period. Rich pulled me aside one day and encouraged me to go get my life insurance license. He said he would be happy to split his commissions with me on my referrals if I did. Sure enough, I studied and passed my life insurance exam with the state of Pennsylvania in August 2003. In September of that year, Rich and I put together my first financial seminar centered on life insurance and real estate. I filled the room with 30 coworkers, friends, and neighbors to attend. Rich explained how life insurance worked, and I explained how I leveraged life insurance to go make a few hundred thousand in the real estate market. Within two months of that seminar, about 25 of my 30 attendees owned cash-value life insurance.

I was excited. I was onto something here. It was difficult for me to focus on my job because all I wanted to do was talk about life insurance.

I wanted to quit my job and sell life insurance full-time. I was 35 years old. My wife and I had just had our fourth child, and we had just moved into a fairly expensive home. Leaving a high-paying job that provided benefits and the security of a weekly paycheck to go sell life insurance, where my income was completely based on commissions, was crazy. But with the support of my wife and the comfort of knowing that I had money in the bank and access to the cash value of my life insurance policy if I needed it, that is exactly what I did on February 1, 2004.

Incidentally, not long after jumping into my new career, I learned about indexed universal life. It was the hot new insurance product that was offered by only a few insurance companies. The more I looked into IUL and how it worked, the more I wanted it for my own portfolio. I was intrigued by the upside potential for my cash value while still being protected from the market's declines. Up until that point, all I owned was whole life insurance. Although whole life performed as I hoped it would the previous 10 years, I wish it could have earned more during the stock market run in the late '90s.

With that in mind, I rolled the cash value of my whole life policy into a new IUL policy in 2004. The IRS allows for you to transfer the cash value from one life insurance policy to another without incurring any tax consequences under what's referred to as a 1035 Exchange. At the time, I was concerned about buying into such a new and unproven product. Fast-forward more than a decade and the jury is in. Transferring my cash value from whole life to IUL was a fantastic decision for me. Let's face it: if you remove 2008 from the equation, which IUL did for me, the market has done terrific since 2004.

Million-Dollar "Stroke of Luck"

One day during the summer of 2005 I went golfing with my neighbor. We got paired up with a guy I had never met before. His name was Pat. Turns out Pat was a real estate broker turned land developer. Back in 2005, everyone wanted to be a land developer. By the third hole Pat was telling me how he and his partners had acquired the rights to 110 acres about five miles up the road. They needed $1 million to develop the land. They were looking for a silent investor. Pat was confident that it could be sold for major profits once it was developed. I was familiar with the area he was talking about. Pat and I met a few times over the next couple weeks to discuss what he was looking to do. I liked what I saw. It was time to raise some money.

By the time all this was happening, I had been selling life insurance for about 18 months. I must have had around 100 clients. I sent an e-mail to all of my clients and encouraged them to attend a meeting to learn about a very qualified real estate investment opportunity with my new friend Pat and his partners.

I had about 50 people show up to our meeting. Pat made a presentation about the opportunity. He covered the huge upside potential. He was confident that his firm could develop the land and simultaneously sign retailers to leases that would then lead to the ability to sell the developed property to a larger organization that specialized in running shopping centers. Pat also covered the risks. This was no slam-dunk investment. They could spend a lot of money on township approvals and trying to get tenants lined up, but there was no assurance any of this would work. Pat and his company needed $1 million from investors to take the risk. If all went well, Pat was confident they could pay back $2–$3 million in a three-year time frame.

When Pat and his team were finished, I stood up, told everyone that the minimum investment was $25,000, and then asked, "Who's in?" About 40 of the 50 attendees raised their hands. Over the next few weeks I worked with an attorney to form a corporation to pool the investors' money, which would end up being used to invest in Pat's project. I ended up raising $1 million from about 30 investors who came up with their money first, which included me. On behalf of the investors, I wrote a $1 million check to Pat's company on October 12, 2005.

Fast-forward three years to September 30, 2008. In the midst of the economic meltdown that was taking place on Wall Street and in the real estate markets around the country, Pat wrote me and my investors a $4 million check! Pat and his company successfully developed the land and sold it off to another company for over $22 million. Our cut was the $4 million they paid us back.

So why am I telling you this story? Eleven of the 30 investors, including myself, used money from the cash-value life insurance policies they purchased from Rich and me the previous five years. A $50,000 investment netted someone about $200,000 back. The 11 investors who used the money from their life insurance policies had no other way to invest. The rest of their money was tied up in 401(k)s and IRAs, and those vehicles were in the process of incurring 30%–40% losses during the 2008 correction.

Are you starting to see the power of liquidity? Remember that 3% of the public is financially independent. They make their money seizing the moment when solid investment opportunities come up, and they always come up. But the only way you can seize the moment is to have funds that are accessible. Cash-value life insurance is the perfect place to accumulate long-term savings that can also be accessed to take advantage of moneymaking opportunities that arise along the way. Savvy investors don't lock money up for 10, 20, and 30 years. That's a strategy for the 97% of people just getting by.

Let IUL Help Buy Your Next Car

When people purchase a car, they typically borrow the money from a bank and pay the bank back over five years. Let's use a $30,000 car financed at 5% over five years. Your monthly payment would be about $560 a month for 60 months. At the end of five years, all you have is car worth $7,000, if you are lucky. Meanwhile, you spent over $33,000 in car payments that you will never see again.

Here is how I buy a $30,000 car. I take $30,000 from my life insurance policy and pay cash for the car. I then send a check for $560 back to the insurance company each month to go back into my policy instead of sending it to a bank. Five years later, I have the same $7,000 car as you, but I also have $33,000 back in my policy. You see, in my eyes, my life insurance policy is my bank.

My car-buying strategy is much better. When I lay it out like this at my financial seminars, people literally grin or their jaws drop because of the epiphany they just realized.

I have four children. Each one of them has an IUL policy that I purchased for them as soon as I got into the business full-time in 2004. If all my kids do is utilize their IUL policy to purchase their vehicles throughout their lifetime, think of how much better off financially they will be as a result.

My point is this: savvy investors don't lock up money for 20–40 years. My IUL policy is my version of a 401(k), except the cash in my policy is liquid. I want access to my money to be able to pounce on investment opportunities that arise. The benefits of IUL are strong enough to own the product even if you never touched the cash value until retirement.

But wouldn't it be nice to know that you could if the right opportunity came up or if a financial hardship arose?

The Times Herald

Businessman has 'stroke of luck' on golf course, receives winning investment tip

Tuesday, December 9, 2008, by GARY PULEO / *Times Herald* Staff

—Dean Vagnozzi might have settled for a few tips on knocking some strokes off his golf game and called it a day.

But his instincts told him the big developer guy and the investment opportunity were the real deal.

Now a much richer man because he met Pat Heller out on the golf course that day, Vagnozzi told his story over lunch at Sullivan's Steak House in King of Prussia recently.

Sitting across the table from him, celebrating the fiscal benefits of the forthcoming Upland Square shopping center, were Heller, Stephen Nave and Greg Newell of Sapphire Development Company headquartered in King of Prussia.

"I never met this guy before and on the first hole I asked him what he did," Vagnozzi recalled, slicing into his meat loaf. "He formed this real estate development company with a few guys he went to high school with because they had the rights to some land."

Two holes later, Heller found out that Vagnozzi worked for Delaware Valley Financial Group and was no stranger to real estate investing.

"They were nickel-and-dime things. I made a few bucks building some houses, but nothing huge," Vagnozzi noted.

By the time the men reached the seventh hole, Heller was explaining that he was looking for investors to share the risk on 110 acres off Route 100 in Pottstown.

"They bought the rights to the land back in September 2005, which was literally right before the real estate market tanked. They had the right to walk away from it but wanted to pursue possibly building a big shopping center with the right guys," Vagnozzi said.

Heller was looking for a million bucks. Vagnozzi made a few calls.

Within the next week, Heller, Nave and Newell presented their sales pitch to about 50 of Vagnozzi's acquaintances. In the end, 28 people came up with the money — a group that included "ordinary" folks, like a police officer, a school teacher and stay-at-home mom.

"The story is that most of the people who invested were ordinary people," Vagnozzi said. "A handful could have afforded to lose it, but most in the group couldn't afford to lose it. They took a gamble and eventually it paid off.

"If you divide a million by 28 . . . some people put in $30,000, some put in $50,000. Two guys put in $10,000 each. At the time we said, 'Don't get involved unless you can afford to lose the money.' People said, 'I hear you, but here's the money anyway.' Thank God it worked out."

Heller had been faced with guys bailing on the project before, so he confessed he was grateful to Vagnozzi for pulling it all together.

"A couple of guys could have written the check by themselves, but they got cold feet on it. The funny part about investing is when it comes time to write the check, people turn and go the other way," Heller said.

"But Dean turned it on full speed and got it done." Nave nodded.

"Dean went to a bunch of people who weren't millionaires and instead of thinking about it forever they decided they wanted in," Nave said. "Nobody really wants to work with 30 people. I was a little leery about having that many investors involved because you never know how the communication will go. Greg and I are engineers. We decided we would go through one point of contact, which would be Dean, and he would get the updates out to all the people."

Vagnozzi fronted $27,000 in legal fees, forming a private placement corporation to oversee the project.

"Looking back, it was probably very risky," he said. "I had 10 percent interest in any profits. We were all very open about it and everybody was OK with it. If we lost our money, we don't make a dime."

With the money finally lining their pockets, the Sapphire guys went on the hunt for a buyer for their 110 acres. "Sure enough, at the end of 2007 they sold the land for $22 million," Vagnozzi said.

Upland Square will be anchored by Target, Best Buy, LA Fitness, Petco, Bed, Bath & Beyond, Chili's, Staples and Giant supermarket, he added.

"To understand the magnitude of what these guys developed, this is basically a 700,000 square foot shopping center," he said.

In March of this year, the investors got their million dollars back and discovered they would soon hit pay dirt, to the tune of $2.9 million.

"We knew the money was coming, we just didn't know when," Vagnozzi remembered. "I would see these people around town and everybody already had the money spent. One guy pulls up in a brand new Lexus and tells me he's got another one at home. My brother bought a new house. I got a pool going in. And we didn't even have the money yet," he added, laughing.

"We gave them the money three years ago and a month later the real estate market starts tanking, so everybody pretty much wanted to hang themselves for the first two years.

"But now our million turned into $3.9 million almost to the day in a three-year time frame."

None of the men at the table had heard of any similar rags-to-riches tales coming from the real estate world in the last few years. "This is a classic American success story about real people," Vagnozzi said.

chapter 12

Assemble a Team

I originally had this as my first chapter. That's how important I feel the lesson is to your finances. I moved it toward the back of the book because I wanted to come out swinging. I thought the best way to get your attention was to trash the financial vehicles that everyone has been told are the be-all, end-all of financial instruments, the 401(k) and IRA. Once I started down that path, it was tough to find the best place to insert my views on putting together a team. I decided to let it be one of the last thoughts you have as you finish this book.

Presidents, CEOs, and Football Coaches

FIGURE 12.1. *President Barack Obama and Vice President Joe Biden pose with the full Cabinet for an official group photo in the Grand Foyer of the White House, July 26, 2012. (Official White House Photo by Chuck Kennedy)*

Consider the photo you see above. This photo is of President Barack Obama and his cabinet. President Obama was the President at the time of the first printing of this book.

The president has a cabinet. CEOs have a board of directors. An NFL head coach has assistant coaches. When it comes to your finances, get yourself a team. One advisor can't possibly have a monopoly on all of the good ideas.

Anyway, the picture shows a president and his cabinet. There are a lot of people who have responsibility to help shape the decisions of the only guy you got to cast a vote for or against. There are over 20 members of a presidential cabinet. Every member has a different area of expertise. Do you think every member of the cabinet gets along? Of course not. Would we want a president making decisions in a vacuum with absolutely no input at all? Would we want major pieces of legislation signed by a man or woman who might not understand some of the details about the legislation because it is not his or her area of expertise? Certainly not. We vote for a president not only for his or her leadership skills but also for his or her ability to build teams of advisors that will help him or her do a better job.

This, maybe obviously, is why it is such a big deal when some more obscure member of the cabinet is involved in some sort of scandal. It reflects on the judgment of the person who put him or her on the team in the first place. We want our presidents to be confident enough to put together a team that has character, will challenge their thought, and not yes them to death.

Read that last sentence again. Why? Because when we get to the part about building our own team, we have to look not only at how we can handle challenges to our own perspective or thought but also at how our key team members will handle challenges to their perspectives and thoughts. Do we want team members who will fight to the death to see their way adhered to, or do we want a team confident enough to arrive at the best decision for the leader to make?

Business Leadership

This concept is not exclusive to elected officials. Just type the search "board of advisors" into Google and spend five minutes looking at the results. You will find article after article about how you should go about building your own board of advisors or directors. Don't stop there. Click over to the "news" section of your Google search and just look at all the announcements about the new board members that have been recently added to companies all over the world.

Boards of advisors or directors exist to give objective input to the leaders of companies. Sometimes the board members know the industry well, sometimes they know related industries well, and sometimes the members of the board know not the industry that the company is operating in but have a very defined expertise or skill that the company values.

Sports Leadership

Business and politics not your thing? OK, then, what about sports? Football, for example, specifically the NFL. I assure you that every head coach in the NFL knows more than enough about every position on the field. Yet, every NFL head coach has a team of 15–20 assistant coaches that help him evaluate players, teach techniques, and put game plans together. It would be crazy imagining an NFL team with one coach. Would you want your home team to have one coach? No way!

Are You "Winging It"?

OK, I think I've made my point, but believe me when I say I could go on and on. The fact is that teams are something that we don't pay much attention to but they are all around us. So let's turn our attention back to your personal finances. Do you have a team? Are you getting input from varying perspectives? The sad truth is that when I ask my seminar attendees whether they work with an advisor, only about 15%–25% of the hands go up. Then I ask the people who have their hands raised whether they get proactive financial advice from more than one person every year. Just about every hand goes down.

That baffles me. When it comes to something as important as your retirement planning, about 75%–85% of people are "winging it," and the rest of the people are working with just one person. Do you see one person in the photograph of the presidents' cabinet? Nope. Does the head coach of your favorite sports team have one assistant coach? Nope. But for some reason, those of you working with an advisor think your guy or gal has a monopoly on all the good ideas. Doesn't that sound ridiculous? And to make things worse, that one guy or gal who you may have as an advisor probably has a stock-market-focused level of expertise that generates income from you regardless of whether you make money. Go figure.

Your Financial Advisory Team

Nobody, including me, has a monopoly on all of the good ideas. That's why you need several advisors with complementary skill sets to provide you with financial advice. You need to be able to have an annual meeting with this team to discuss your finances. Every advisor on your team should be comfortable with sharing his or her recommendations for you with your other advisors. You are not looking for a debate at these meetings, but you want to know each advisor's perspective on certain topics. Ultimately, it is up to you to determine what financial strategies to implement and what financial products to acquire in order to help you achieve your goals.

Your team should be made up of no fewer than four separate individuals. All of them play an equally important role.

The first "must-have" team member would be someone who has a securities license. This advisor has a strong understanding of the stock market and other investments that are classified as securities such as mutual funds. "Huh? What gives, Dean? You just spent the past 10 chapters ripping the stock market; now you are saying the first member of our financial team should be someone who specializes in this area."

Let me be clear: nowhere in this book have I said you shouldn't have money tied to the stock market. Personally speaking, I don't have any money in a 401(k) or IRA, but I do have an account with an online broker where I own one stock that has paid a 9% dividend for the past few years. That being stated, I don't expect anyone reading this book to go from having all of his or her money in the market to getting out of it completely. My message is this: traditional investing is nowhere near as good as you have been told it is. Not even close! As a result, I don't feel you should have anywhere near the amount of money tied to Wall Street that you probably do. In addition, the other main theme is that if you simply make indexed universal life 25%–50% of your portfolio, you will enjoy all of the benefits we have covered thus far.

How much of your money should be tied to the market? Your guess is as good as mine. It depends on many things, such as age, risk tolerance, and how well your other investments are doing. I've heard a rule of thumb that you should take your age and have the same amount of money OUT of the market. So if you are 45, then you should have 45% of your money outside of the market and 55% IN the market. I'm 47 as I type this. Do I have 47% of my money outside of the market? No, not even close. About 95% of my money is out of the market. But I don't expect you to do the same, at least not right away.

You can find securities-licensed advisors at companies such as Merrill Lynch, Ameriprise, and Morgan Stanley. There are plenty of other qualified individuals who work for smaller firms as well or who have their own businesses representing broker dealers and registered investment advisors that you have never heard of.

A big reason why I want you to include one of these traditional advisors in your team is because this person has access to more investments than just mutual funds. There are investments that are classified as securities that are not mutual funds. These "alternative" investments have nice upside potential and may not have the same downside exposure as a traditional mutual fund. One example would be a real estate investment trust, commonly referred to as a REIT. A REIT is a company that owns and in most cases operates income-producing real estate. REITs own many types of commercial real estate, ranging from office and apartment buildings to warehouses, hospitals, shopping centers, hotels, and even timberlands. A REIT has its own list of benefits and risks for you to evaluate, but I hope you see my point. A good securities-licensed advisor should be able to put several alternative investments in front of you like a REIT. Make this advisor earn his or her money.

If all of your market-related investments are going to be in mutual funds, then you should seriously consider opening an online trading account and purchasing indexed funds. There is plenty of research that suggests that indexed funds outperform most mutual fund managers, and you won't have to pay an advisor to purchase them. You can call a company such as Vanguard and work with one of its in-house advisors who can help you allocate your mutual fund portfolio using its funds for minimal fees.

The next "must-have" advisor on your team should be, surprise, surprise, an insurance expert. I specifically mean someone who is an expert on life insurance, annuities, disability insurance, and long-term-care insurance. I'm not referring to a property and casualty (P&C) insurance advisor who focuses on homeowner and car insurance. Property and casualty insurance advisors can sell life insurance, for example, but their main focus is homeowner and auto policies. Maybe you do indeed have a P&C agent who truly understands cash-value life insurance. If that is the case, great, but make sure he or she has access to indexed universal life. Some companies such as State Farm do not offer IUL and do not allow their representatives to sell any life insurance other than the products that they offer.

To maximize wealth, you want an insurance professional who truly understands how cash-value life insurance works and how it needs to be properly designed to maximize financial growth and minimize financial risk. But A Better Financial Plan isn't just about growing your money. It's also about protecting yourself from unexpected financial and health-related hardships.

Let me make my point with term life insurance. In the past 10 years, I have come across just one client who actually came into my office with adequate life insurance coverage. JUST ONE! Everyone I meet THINKS he or she has the proper amounts of life insurance, but very few actually do. The sad truth is that just about every family out there spends more money per month on their cable bill than they do on the proper amounts of life insurance. Do you? If so, then I strongly suggest that you reevaluate your financial priorities. The consequences to your family in the event of your early death are catastrophic, both emotionally and financially. A strong financial plan is one that works in good times and bad. How much life insurance should you have? A good rule of thumb is to have enough coverage to replace your current income from now until age 65 at least. Disability coverage is the other major type of insurance coverage that everyone neglects. If you have disability coverage only through your employer, then you likely need more. The disability coverage you get at work typically covers 65% of your salary only. Could you live off 65% of your salary? Bet you can't. That's why you need a disability policy outside of work. Have I made my point? If all you did after reading this book is went out and bought the proper amounts of cheap term life insurance and/or a disability policy to protect your loved ones, then I've helped you.

Let's get back to the reasoning for why you need both a stockbroker and an insurance advisor. You will SELDOM find someone who focuses on the stock market who truly understands the insurance industry and the products it offers. VERY SELDOM. Stockbrokers usually have an insurance license, but very few of them understand the products that the insurance industry offers; however, most act like they do. The same is true for the insurance advisor. He or she may very well have a securities license to sell investments such as mutual funds, but I don't know many who are really good at it, yet they too will act like they are.

Advisors in the financial services industry are very protective and don't like to admit that they don't know everything about every financial product. The last thing most of them want to do is work with other advisors. They are all fearful that the other advisor will steal their clients from them. Well, guess what? That's their problem, not yours. Make sure you get an expert securities-licensed agents and a solid life insurance expert. They complement each other well. The securities industry and its advisors have an "I can get you a better, higher rate of return over time" attitude. The insurance industry and its agents have a "your money is safer, more tax efficient, easier to manage with us" attitude.

You need both. Don't let anyone tell you otherwise. Both types of advisors will offer you products and perspectives that are unique to each industry and will complement each other extremely well.

The third "must-have" advisor is an accountant. If you are still doing your own taxes by using some cheap version of Quicken software, then you might want to consider employing the help of an accountant. If you are already using one, then what questions are you asking of him or her? A big mistake people make is to use their accountant only to help with the previous year's tax returns. They forget that an accountant's perspective is predominantly one of hindsight: what have you done with your money, and what are the tax implications? I encourage you to ask your accountant his or her opinion of your financial moves before you make them, not after.

Let me give you a quick example. A friend of mine went out on his own doing some consulting work and was being paid as an independent contractor. What he didn't know is that as an independent contractor, he was responsible for an employment tax of sorts on his income. He could have lowered this tax burden by incorporating, something his accountant told him when he was filling out the prior year's tax return. Had he had the accountant on his team, he would have run his new venture by him and would have been made aware of this option before setting out. He would have saved thousands of dollars.

Accountants are considered the most trusted type of financial advisor. They obviously have a broad understanding of most financial instruments out there. This general knowledge allows them to ask questions of your other advisors that you may not know to ask. That's good. The flip side of that is that most accountants are experts on tax-related issues. They are not necessarily experts on stocks, bonds, mutual funds, life insurance, or long-term-care insurance. Many people think they are, and, as a result, the accountant is asked his or her opinion on the recommendations of the other advisors. Your accountant may not come right out and admit that he or she is not an expert on the products you are asking his or her opinion of. My own accountant has confessed this to me. My own accountant has said, "Dean, my clients ask me about life insurance, mutual funds, municipal bonds, 529 plans, and financial aid—you name it." My accountant doesn't know the first thing about the college financial aid process, yet so many of his clients think he does. If you are going to ask the accountant his or her opinion of the recommendations of your other advisors, I suggest you do so in the presence of the other advisors or at least give the recommending advisors a chance to respond to the comments of the accountant.

The fourth "must-have" advisor is an attorney. Out of the four, I admit that an attorney will likely give you the least amount of proactive financial advice. I'm not suggesting that you call your attorney and ask him or her about what mutual funds you should buy or what kind of life insurance you should own. A good attorney, however, will give you a perspective on things that the others on your team can't or won't. Let's face it: an attorney is usually called when you need help to get out of trouble. Examples include getting help after a car accident or a DUI. Perhaps you've been sued for one reason or another and you need representation. If you are going through a divorce, you call an attorney. These are all great reasons to work with an attorney, but they are all reactive reasons. Moving forward, I want you to be proactive. I don't make a major financial decision that is outside of my expertise unless I consult with my attorney, just to get his perspective. My attorney is very conservative. I want his opinion to help keep me from making bad investments. It's a lot cheaper to pay him for an hour or two of his time to get some sound advice than it is to pay him for 50 hours to get me out of a bad deal. Attorneys have seen and heard a million horror stories that they can share with you to help you avoid the costly mistakes that their other clients have made.

That being said, it's up to you determine what financial moves you make. Get advice from the four advisors I just mentioned but, ultimately, you need to do what you feel is best.

To make my point, let me tell you about a time I *ignored* my attorney's advice. As I briefly told you about in chapter 11, I made a few bucks during the real estate boom a few years back. In the midst of my real estate dabblings, I had an opportunity to purchase some land not far from my home and build four homes. The land was for sale by a builder who would sell me the building lots only if I hired him to build the homes. I spent a good deal of time discussing this potential purchase with the builder and developed a strong comfort level with him. I spoke to a few realtors about the potential value of the homes once built. I thought I could make a nice profit with little downside due to the hot real estate market. I decided to move forward with the purchase. The builder drafted some contracts for me to review. I invited my attorney to lunch with me to meet the builder and discuss the project. In short, my attorney didn't get a good vibe from this builder. He thought his contract was poorly written and advised me not to move forward. He didn't think it was worth the risk.

I gave my attorney's recommendation a lot of thought but still decided to move forward—after heading some of my attorney's advice and tweaking some of the contract terms. I had done my homework and was confident that I was making a good decision. Bottom line: everything worked out just fine. Four homes were constructed fairly quickly, and all were sold within two months of completion. I made over $150,000 as a result of going with my instincts.

In summary, *just like the president, a CEO, or a head football coach, assemble a team of advisors. Put them all together in a room at least once a year to discuss your finances. If you don't get your team together to openly discuss your finances, you run the risk of receiving conflicting input that causes you to make decisions based on inaccurate information. That is the only way to flush out what is truly in your best interest.*

chapter 13

Fiction, Facts, and Next Steps

In a perfect world, you've read this book start to finish with an open mind, ready to learn new things to improve your finances. I'm also hoping that you read the entire book without asking anyone else's opinion along the way. This book is a written version of the educational financial seminars that I have conducted since 2004.

I am extremely confident that you nodded in agreement as I laid out the other side of the story pertaining to the 401(k) and IRA, as well as my commentary on things such as the recurring revenue model of Wall Street. It is also very likely that you were impressed with Tom's IUL statement and how the cash values went up 7% in value during the same period of time that the S&P 500 dropped almost 10%. Then there were Phil's statements. When Phil was 69, his IUL policy earned around 10% the previous year while having had no risk of stock-market-related losses.

But as you saw, Phil's annual IUL statement got even better when he was 72. He earned 21% on his cash value. Both annual statements prove that Phil's annual insurance-related policy charges are significantly less than what his tax bill would have been if he earned those yields in a nonqualified brokerage account. I know you liked what you saw there.

How about the case I made for how IUL will consistently credit 6.5%–8.5% over any 5-, 10-, 20-, 30-, or 40-year time horizon, using past performance data from the S&P 500? You had to have found this compelling.

In chapter 9 I taught you how to become couple B. The simple strategy of making IUL a 25%–50% piece of your portfolio will allow you to cut your tax bill in half while you spend and enjoy 50% more money during retirement. That had to have been a major eye-opener for you.

Finally, chapter 11 introduced the benefits of treating IUL as your own personal bank. IUL is a long-term-savings vehicle that simultaneously provides liquidity to you when an investment opportunity comes up or a hardship arises while allowing you the ability to eliminate the need to borrow money from a bank. Who can disagree with the logic of any of that?

I am extremely confident that you like what you read and saw in this book because not only is it common sense but also I have laid this out for thousands of seminar attendees since 2004 and they all have the same "blown-away" look in their eyes as I present this information to them.

Unfortunately, I am just as confident that as soon as you discuss with others what you've learned in this book, you're going to get a lot of funny looks. After the funny looks, you are going to be told you are crazy. And as sure as the sun will rise tomorrow, if you are told you are crazy from enough friends and financial experts, you will quickly forget everything I proved to you in this book as if you never read it, for fear that you've been misled somehow. If an advisor who has experience in selling IUL gave you this book, that advisor knows exactly what I am talking about.

In an effort to help take the wind out of the sails of any noise or false information you hear from your friends or financial experts in the media pertaining to IUL, I am going to provide you with answers to a few of the more common misconceptions. Obviously, you have an entire book full of evidence to dispute whatever incorrect statements you hear, but I thought I'd help address the more popular comments now.

Let me start with a real-life e-mail that I received from Darren, back in June of 2013. This is such a classic example of everything I've covered in this chapter and a perfect example of why you need to assemble a team of advisors and occasionally put them all in a room together.

Darren and his wife attended one of my seminars in early May of 2013. Like most of my attendees, he was impressed with what I covered and requested to meet with me one-on-one to see whether I could improve their finances.

In short, Darren and his wife were both around 50 years of age and financially resembled so many couples that I see in my office. A good bit of their money was tied up in their current 401(k)s and IRAs from previous jobs. They expressed how their 401(k)s and IRAs had just gotten back to the levels they had been at prior to the crash of 2008 but were mad that it took almost five years to do so. They were also saving money each month with an advisor they had met a few years back who worked for one of the large brokerage houses. They were leery of another market correction and hated the fact that so much of their retirement dollars were in vehicles that went up and down with the stock market. They didn't know what else to do with their money. Oh, and they conceded they didn't have enough life insurance. I'm leaving a bunch of stuff out, I'm sure, but that's enough for now.

Toward the end of our first meeting, I gave this couple a high-level overview of IUL and how it could be used to complement the rest of their portfolio. Now, to be fair, I did not cover everything with them that I covered in this book. Our meeting had gone long enough, and I thought we could cover the rest at our next meeting.

From: Darren [xxxxxxxx@comcast.net]
Sent: Wednesday, June 05, 2013 1:29 PM
To: Dean Vagnozzi
Subject: IUL Update

Dean,

After extensive due diligence, Univ. Index Life Ins is not for us.

The fees are too high; the product should not be used as an investment vehicle and it is portrayed as such; dividends from the index don't get credited; the insurance co can make changes during the life of the policy to benefit them, etc, etc. I understand the product has some positives, but not enough for me. In addition, even if I was interested, which I'm not at this time, we can get a better guaranteed minimum rate on the open market.

Right now, we are comfortable with our present investments and if anything changes, I will certainly give you a call.

Regards,

Darren

Darren and his wife were excited about what they had learned about IUL thus far and eagerly set another meeting with me for the following week so that I could finish educating them on IUL and how it works.

A few days later, I received this e-mail from Darren. Take a look:

Just like that, they changed their mind about IUL and canceled our upcoming meeting. I could tell from the e-mail they sent and by the way they phrased things that they either read something on the Internet or spoke to someone who knew just enough about IUL to be dangerous.

After I received this e-mail, I picked up the phone and gave Darren a call. He confessed that he called his current advisor and everything he put in the e-mail was from the notes he took while on the phone with his guy. I encouraged Darren to come sit with me again to get the rest of the IUL story so that he could make up his own mind based on all of the facts. He agreed.

Let's examine the e-mail Darren sent that summarizes beautifully some of the outdated or inaccurate information about IUL that you may hear as well.

"The fees are too high"

You have to ask, "Compared to what?" Yes, the fees and expenses with cash-value life insurance are indeed high compared to the fees within a mutual fund or most other traditional investments. But when you look at the big picture, which you have to do in order to make a fair comparison, insurance-related expenses are a bargain compared to mutual fund fees, advisor fees, term insurance, and taxes. It's that simple. I'd gladly pay 10% of my premiums to insurance costs to avoid paying 28%, 33%, or 35% in taxes. It's a simple math equation. If there was ever a penny-wise, pound-foolish way of thinking, it is avoiding insurance costs to pay taxes. How about considering what many of the fees are paying for, such as preventing you from losing money? Isn't that worth something? It sure is. Refer to chapter 7 for my comparison of insurance costs for a 69 and 72-year-old-man versus mutual fund fees, advisor fees, term insurance, and taxes.

"The product should not be used as an investment vehicle"

There are several commonsense answers to this statement. Let's start with the non-argumentative response. OK, don't use IUL as an investment. Simply transfer a piece of your safe money into IUL. Your safe portfolio is likely not earning much, so why not put a chunk of it into cash-value life insurance? Treat IUL as a multi-beneficial savings vehicle. End of debate.

Now, if you want a debate with whoever makes this comment to you, I would ask, "Why not?" This outdated way of thinking refers to when whole life insurance was the only form of cash-value insurance. That was 40 years ago. Life insurance has evolved, as I covered in chapter 4, and most people have no idea how IUL works or how it is different from its much more conservative ancestor, whole life. Perhaps the originator of this thinking feels that in order to be classified as an investment vehicle, the product must have the ability to lose money. Perhaps the originator of this thinking believes that a true investment vehicle needs volatility. Who knows?

Having typed that last paragraph, let me give you some friendly advice. Do your best to avoid this "insurance as an investment" debate with someone if you can. There is no way to change someone's mind about how life insurance works, specifically IUL, in a few minutes. So don't try. Someone needs to take the time to read a book like this or spend 45 minutes to an hour with a life insurance expert to learn about IUL. If that person won't take the time to learn, then nothing you say will convince him or her that you know what you are doing by purchasing an IUL policy.

"Dividends from the index don't get credited"

Correct, they don't. Are dividends credited toward annuities? No. Are dividends credited toward CDs and money market accounts? No. Are they credited toward any safe piece of your portfolio? No, they are not. Does the lack of a dividend payment make a financial vehicle a bad piece of your portfolio? Of course not. Which product would you rather have had in 2008, a blue-chip stock that paid a high dividend that dropped 35% of its value or tax-free life insurance cash values that never lost a penny? Dividends are great, but the lack of them doesn't make something a bad piece of your portfolio, nor does their presence make something a good investment.

"The insurance company can make changes during the life of the policy to benefit itself"

I love this one. I really do. If there was ever a fact that was misrepresented by traditional advisors, it's this one. Yes, insurance companies can change a few things within the policy each year, such as the mortality costs and the index caps. Traditional advisors spin that to sound like a negative. The fact that an insurance company can tweak the policy is very good for you, not bad. Let me explain.

In the case of mortality costs, ask yourself, are people living longer or shorter? Longer! So if people are living longer, your insurance costs are becoming smaller over time, not larger. You want the insurance company to be able to drop the amount of the mortality costs it charges you. Insurance companies are just like every other company. They are trying to make the best product they can to beat their competition and to attract new clients. The insurance company that increases mortality expenses within its policies as people are living longer will be out of business fast. Keep in mind that insurance agents have the ability to sell life insurance with hundreds of companies. If an insurance company jacks up the fees and expenses of its policyholders, word will get out and agents will stop selling the company's insurance products. Since I came into the business full-time in 2004, I am not aware of any insurance company that has increased the mortality charges of any of my clients.

As for the index caps that can be changed once a year, this is another positive—a very big positive. The 10%–14% caps that most IUL policies have are tied to interest rates. Life insurance companies make money by investing their long-term investment portfolios in interest-rate-sensitive investments. They take some of their annual profits and buy options to cover the index crediting on IUL policies. As everyone knows, interest rates are at historic lows as I type this. There is only one way for interest rates to go, and that is up. As interest rates rise, so will the portfolio profits for the insurance companies. As their profits rise, the insurance companies are able to spend more money on options to cover the index crediting on their IUL policies. The more money they spend on options, the higher the caps will rise. An insurance company that has 13% caps today will likely increase its caps to 14% or 15%. It has to increase caps as interest rates rise, because competitors will be doing the same thing.

Think about it. Can't a traditional advisor increase the fees that he or she charges clients? Yes. Can't a mutual fund manager increase the fees inside the mutual fund? Of course he or she can. Take any business, for that matter. Doesn't the management at Domino's Pizza reserve the right to double the price of their pizzas? Of course they do. So why don't they? Because their competitors keep them honest. Domino's Pizza won't stay in business long if it charges 25% more money for a pizza than Papa John's Pizza, even though it reserves the right to. Well, it is the same thing with the insurance industry. Remember that an insurance company being able to tweak things such as fees and caps is a good thing. No question about it.

"I understand the product has some positives but not enough for me"

Darren wrote this before he truly understood how IUL worked. When he agreed to come back into my office the following week, we covered just about everything written in this book, and I addressed everything he wrote in his e-mail. Needless to say, Darren owns a large IUL policy today.

Next Steps

Over the years, I have heard every single objection you can think of pertaining to owning cash-value life insurance. As a result, I am fairly certain that every negative thing you will ever hear can be refuted in the pages of this book. The negative comments I hear center on the low returns and inflexibility that come with whole life insurance, not IUL. This inaccurate information generally comes from other advisors who are about to have their clients pull money from them so that they can role it into an IUL policy with me. That was the case with Darren. These traditional agent are, for the most part, protecting their income. You can't blame them, but you also can't make their problems yours.

As I mentioned in the previous chapter, if you value someone's financial opinion, put him or her in the same room with your life insurance agent. Whether it is your accountant, your broker, or your best friend, the only way you'll separate fact from opinion is to put everyone in the same room. If they truly care about helping you, they will be happy to all get together. It also wouldn't be a bad idea to give all of them a copy of this book before the meeting so everyone can get on the same page.

Life insurance has evolved drastically over the past 30 years. Indexed universal life has brought the life insurance industry into the twenty-first century, and it is here to stay. IUL is by far the fastest-growing segment of the life insurance market. Ten years ago, only a few insurance companies offered IUL. Today, more than 100 companies offer IUL, with dozens more planning to roll it out over the next couple of years.

Do you want A Better Financial Plan? If so, then your next step is to seek out a life insurance expert and make indexed universal life 25%–50% of your portfolio, and you will instantly have just that.

About the Author

Kelly O'Keefe Photography

Dean Vagnozzi is not your typical financial professional. He'll suggest you avoid your company's 401(k). He'll tell you not to pay off your mortgage. He'll advise you to forego an IRA. He'll hit you with numerous ideas, none of which you've ever heard your current money manager utter.

Most importantly, he'll make you wealthier than you ever thought possible. Vagnozzi, a 50-year-old financial entrepreneur and president of A Better Financial Plan believes in making your money work hard for you right NOW. If it's locked up in retirement accounts or used to pay ahead on your mortgage, it can't be accessed until much later in life . . . and sitting around waiting is just not Vagnozzi's style.

A 1990 graduate of Albright College, Vagnozzi began his career in accounting, his major field of study. After three months, Vagnozzi knew the repetitive, number-crunching, solitary profession was not for him. A natural enthusiasm and magnetic energy eventually led Vagnozzi to a successful sales career at SAP, Deloitte Consulting, and Anderson, which allowed him to save and explore creative investment strategies. The opportunity to forge his own financial destiny prompted Vagnozzi to begin studying wealth management in earnest, enrolling in seminars, reading books, and researching unorthodox money management tactics. Testing his unique ideas on his own accounts proved successful and excited Vagnozzi in a way his previous career path had not. Following his true calling, in 2004 Vagnozzi quit the rigors of corporate America cold turkey and struck out on his own to form his own financial planning firm in 2004.

Touting his own matchless brand of unconventional investing, Vagnozzi quickly amassed a significant client base made up of smart investors who, like himself, could see there was a better way to achieve a lucrative retirement than the typical cookie-cutter plans. Vagnozzi holds his knowledge close to his vest, saving his best information and ideas for clients. *A Better Financial Plan* outlines the thinking behind Vagnozzi's successful nontraditional strategies. This book will pique any potential investor's interest while clearly showing the passion and energy that have driven Vagnozzi to become the thriving entrepreneur he is today. Vagnozzi and his wife, Christa, live in Collegeville, PA. Parenting his four children—two girls and two boys between the ages of 15 and 22—leaves little time for personal extracurricular activities; however, Vagnozzi wouldn't have it any other way. When he does have some precious spare time, Vagnozzi can be found on the golf course or relaxing by his pool.